THE
DIGNITY
OF SERVICE

THE DIGNITY OF SERVICE

THE POWER OF SOCIAL ENTREPRENEURSHIP

NATHAN W MCKIE WITH JEFFREY BAKER

KS

Kravitz & Sons

INNOVATORS IN PUBLISHING, MARKETING AND ADVERTISING

Kravitz and Sons LLC
204 E Arlington Blvd. Suite B
Greenville, NC 27858

Published by Kravitz and Sons LLC.

ISBN: 979-8-89639-396-2 (sc)
ISBN: 979-8-89639-395-5 (e)

Library of Congress Control Number: In Progress

TABLE OF CONTENTS

PREFACE

Dignity is an interesting word in many ways. Probably most of us don't use it much in our conversations. Once upon a time, there was a lot of emphasis on being dignified. Other than royalty (real or pretend) it is not the gold standard that most people seek. However, it is important to note that once a person has lost their dignity, many characteristics have fallen by the wayside. Once sought-after standards just don't seem that important anymore.

Thankfully, many of us still believe that we are all rightfully due to some dignity. Whatever they lose is on them, and it shouldn't be OK for another person to take it away from them. Oh, but it happens; all the time. So, is it fair to say that those of us who care about it should be allowed to participate in the restoration of it? There are those, of course, who would just as soon forget about it; but we are all less of what we can be when we help perpetuate the situation.

Nathan's background includes entrepreneurship in both forprofit and nonprofit ventures, as well as, participating in several mission trip experiences. Richard Branson said: "Capitalism–which in its purest form is entrepreneurism even among the poorest of the poor – does work; but those who make money from it should put it back into society, not just sit on it as if they are hatching eggs." It is sayings like this that caused him to rethink the matter of service as it relates to poverty. When Jeff was with the Office of Creative Ministries in the Missouri Conference of the United Methodist Church, he brought in Robert Lupton, author of *Toxic Charity: How Churches and Charities Hurt Those They Help (and How to Reverse It)*. His first "commandment" is: you should never do something for someone that they can and should do for themselves. Further, when you do, you rob that person of their *dignity* and create a sense of dependency.

In 2018, Nathan published a book entitled, *The Dignity of Profit: Building Community through Entrepreneurship.* Honestly, promotion was lacking, partially because his wife died a couple of months after the book was published. In addition, he was in the early stages of getting a major project off the ground. We'll go into that later, but we believe it was God's way of forcing him to learn more about the effort. Here we are about two years after releasing that book, and we have learned so much more about what is involved.

There are others who have isolated projects that are somewhat similar to what we are doing. Each situation is unique in its own way, so please don't feel that this is just another version of the others. You should see what we mean as you work your way through the book. Believe us when we tell you: Nathan is more of an enterpriser than an entrepreneur. There's a lot more to be included here about entrepreneurship, so let us just say that an *enterpriser* is one who helps get the ideas of an innovator connected with an entrepreneur. That might seem like a *middle man*, reviled by many salespeople who want to make it seem like they are saving you big bucks by eliminating these pariahs. Bear with us, and we hope we can make a clear distinction.

In any case, the experience has helped us understand the potholes that await anyone who seeks to step out in faith. Don't get us wrong, we are not trying to make the path so clear that anyone will want to do this. What is important, in our view, is that you understand what you will face. In that way, you will be better prepared to get involved rather than run from the situation.

Profit was directed toward churches, and to some degree businesspeople, who weren't that interested in either social enterprises or social entrepreneurship. For the churches' part, business seems too secular to get engaged in (albeit that they actually do it all the time). This goes for civic foundations as well. They don't make the connection between the world of commerce and money has to be the engine that drives programs and facilities management. With that being the case, they certainly have a distaste for supporting for-profit endeavors. We think there was a plausible case made for them getting involved, but we also think the next phase of the project has to be the most important aspect –learning how to be servant leaders.

If we do choose to try to make major changes in our world, where do we start, and how effective can we expect to be? Jeff recently posed the important question: what are we really expecting to accomplish? Good one, but a real stinger! Without that, however, we only have one main thing to bring to the table: more discussion about the status quo without any real solutions. It was staring us in the face, but his question moved it to the top of the heap. It was, of course, what we were really about, but we were only looking at the *what* and the *how*. Vitally important, but insufficient without the major question: Why?

It would be fairly easy to brush the discussion aside with the high goal of alleviating poverty. Certainly, this would not suffice for all we have experienced. It would be like turning a cold shoulder to the problem. So, what are we going to do about it? We're going to give you the benefit of some soul-searching that we did.

First, we are going to admit that alone, we can't really do much toward alleviating poverty or even *moving the poverty needle*. What we can do, however, is to do all we can to raise the level of awareness as to how to make a difference. Second, we know that community development is a major key factor in accomplishing very much. So, we are going to provide some recommendations as to how that can be conducted successfully. Third, in the process, we expect to have as many folks as possible, energized to go out and take on the challenge.

Where do we start? Right, where we will end: asking the big questions. The major one has to be the *Why* one mentioned earlier. The notion of finding something compelling enough to get you involved will be fully exploited. You must first buy into the belief that all of us are created for a purpose and accept that we can help you determine what that is.

Next, we will help get you directed toward some areas you can start to live in. Our giftedness can only flourish if we accept the responsibility we have and get involved where we can make a difference in our lives, the lives of others, and the larger community as well. Along the way, we sprinkle in how to deal with some roadblocks and setbacks that are lurking out there. Perseverance is a necessary component to be faithful to our calling.

When we start to wrap this up for this stage of your game, we will acquaint you with the big question to take out into the playing field (keeping that metaphor going). Spoiler alert: that question is, *What if?* As we present you with opportunities and you discover them yourself along the way, you will need to embrace this notion. That is: making your endeavor successful for you and for those you seek to serve requires that you find your *niche.*

As this is being written, we are still dealing with the COVID-19 pandemic. The rules have gone out the window in many ways. We are in uncharted territory. This situation calls for entrepreneurs who are able to seek out new opportunities and exploit them to the fullest. We have been in a virtual classroom for months now, and it may go on for many more. People have stepped up with heroic efforts and creative solutions. We will need many people who will ask *What if* and find ways to offer paths to a bright future.

It is our prayer that we can offer some solutions even if we can't move the needle. Poverty hurts all, and we must find ways to restore dignity to those who have had it taken away.

INTRODUCTION

The Spring of 2020 will always be remembered as the season of COVID-19, the coronavirus pandemic. You would have to be over 100 years old to have been alive when the most previous and most deadly pandemic occurred. It was the Spanish flu in 1918-1919, and it infected one-third of the world's population. By some estimates, upwards of 40 million people died. COVID19 is still around at this writing and may still be when the book is published. Solid answers escape us at this point, but it doesn't seem that the number of infections or deaths will reach anything like the most previous one.

For many reasons, events like this help to make us better equipped to deal with future ones. This is a pandemic because it spread so rapidly around the globe. In addition to the death toll, the impact on economies around the world has been astounding. Certainly, the effect there will last much longer than the health issues. That's not to minimize the death toll, but we do rely on our ability to attain the means to pay for food, housing, and medicine. Even doctors admit that medicine many times takes a back seat when funds are inadequate.

Start with the *Why*

Richard Branson said: "There is no point in starting your own business unless you do it out of a sense of **frustration**." That might seem a bit counter-intuitive, but many of our business start-ups have begun that way. Nathan's latest, Luke 16 Corp, is his first non-profit venture. It clearly started out of the frustration he faced in getting others to take it on. Admittedly, it needs to be taken over by others, but that is an on-going process. We will address it in more detail later.

If you think about it, it really makes sense that *Why* comes first, or at least side-by-side with *What*. While the frustration is with the *what*, getting involved in it is because of the *why*. If you had a problem to solve, the frustration is with that problem. You want to get involved because of a passion or strong feeling to fix the problem or do something entirely different. You may not even know what until you have done some research or experimentation to see what would work. As long as there is a why, you will probably keep seeking a *what*. Even after you have researched the *what*; the *how*, the *when*, and/or the *where* may send you back to find a *different what*.

You may be completely confused at this point, but you need to stay focused on the *why*. Unless you can satisfy that nagging question, you may be at the end of the quest. Your enthusiasm may have waned into oblivion.

Our Approach

Let's develop the notion that servants are not weak or ignorant folks who can't or won't do any better with themselves. Perhaps you have already come to that conclusion, but hopefully, this book can help you figure out how to be effective in engaging others in the program. As we look at what it means to be a servant leader, we hope you will find yourself imagining how you can pursue your dream or objective with this approach.

Profit was a bit wordy, to be fair. Nathan's objective was to try to dispel any doubts about the approach. It was not designed to spell out the process in a specific way. What he has decided to do is to extract the parts that support the thesis of service for this book. Some of the environmental concepts will be left to either reading of *Profit* or being a part of a study that includes the rest of the concepts therein provided.

There will be a great emphasis on the examples of how other approaches have been right or wrong. It is not our intent to be overly critical; we just want to present an honest look at how others have fared.

Ultimately, the main focus still has to be on developing the community. For we believe that only by doing so can there be a meaningful impact on helping to alleviate poverty. For sure, the effect of the poverty faced in the U.S. and much of the rest of the world is to drain economies of the ability to thrive rather than just striving to keep their heads above water. Robert Lupton, the author of another great book on charity (Charity Detox) refers to efforts to "move the poverty needle". We find that to be a compelling approach. He accurately describes the landscape as it relates to efforts to make an impact. We will look closely at the fallacy of such programs and provide some alternatives that can be very effective.

The Impact of Current Events

When we started this book in 2019, the situation was quite different from what we have experienced since the beginning of 2020. Nathan is a *baby-boomer* and has been involved in business most of his life. His father and mother lived through the Great Depression and World War What they experienced shaped their lives in terms of how they treated any wealth that they accumulated. Vicariously, it affected Nathan to some degree. He and most of his contemporaries couldn't appreciate the shortages their parents had to endure.

The 1960s were a tumultuous time as baby boomers started coming of age. Most of their parents wanted to spare their children the difficulties they suffered. The Vietnam War divided the country like nothing had since the Civil War. Racial strife was a part of the mix as well. While the economy of the country was beginning to run on all cylinders, socially and politically, the divide became greater. The lines began to be drawn generationally. The experiences that had shaped the *Greatest Generation* (those who lived during World War II) were not transferred into the values of their children. For almost all of the disparate groups, a sense of entitlement pervaded the country.

Subsequent generations rejected any title that was laid on them, but there were distinctive characteristics, nonetheless. We will delve into that somewhat later, but the point is: the work ethic that permeated many of the younger people prior to the *pandemic* of 2020 (and maybe beyond) has caused a drain on our economy and retarded the growth of the recovery of the Trump administration to date. Many would say that the growth experienced was much greater than ever before. However, the inability to maximize production has been directly linked to a lack of desire to work for a living. Paying people not to work had reached a level that no one could have anticipated.

Since we can't predict the future with much accuracy at all these days, we must adhere to principles that are timeless. We must love God and our neighbor. We must learn how to live in a community so that we work together to make this world better than before. If we only survive, we will be back in the same situation as we are now very shortly. We must learn from our mistakes and failures and remember that we can only achieve what we are purposed for if we trust God in everything we do. We have placed these thoughts at this point in the book because everything we say from here on depends on your believing this.

If you don't accept this now, please continue with an open mind. We are in this together as members of the human race. There will be pain for a while, but nothing really great has been achieved without it. A.W. Tozer said, "It is doubtful that God can bless a man until He hurts him deeply." After all, it is times like this that show our true character. As we look back on this, we will no doubt find many ways that life is better. It has been said that we live life moving forward, but we can only understand it by looking backward at what has occurred. When we do, we may not readily realize the good, but it is there. Either way, it is something that we need to happen at this juncture.

A recommendation that Nathan accepted many years ago is *journaling*. This is the practice of making note of things that happen to us as we experience life. It could be an observation, something that someone said, a song you heard, or perhaps an opportunity that you chose to pursue (or not). The context will be important because every memory is contextual. Recalling events that you have recorded can be very cathartic. Robert Lupton often says that we should never treat something chronic as if it were a crisis. How we deal with those is quite different, mainly because we like to see light at the end of the tunnel when we are dealing with a crisis. We become anxious when we are in the middle of one, such as the COVID-19 virus. Chronic situations, such as poverty, call for a quite different approach.

In all likelihood, we will be past the virus by the time this book is complete. In the transition from the crisis to some sense of normalcy (if there can be such a thing now), we can hopefully take some time to look back over our notes and begin to find a pathway into our future that makes sense. We'll not know a lot about this side of Heaven, but we need to come to some peace with it all. We already see some attempts to help us do that. Becoming a healthy person can be critical to moving on.

So, here are some things that we should take notice of:

- Most predictions will be much higher than is realistic for things such as the number of people who contract the virus, the number of people who die from it, etc.

- A lot of money will be thrown at the problems created by the virus, and some people will try to deal with some of the chronic problems (like poverty) as part of the true crisis. In the end, many of the people who need help will not receive it.

- Some people will panic; some will dismiss much of this as hyperbole or some kind of conspiracy. There are motives behind being extreme in either case.

- There will be some genuine heroes, and there will be those who try to *grab the glory* who aren't heroes at all.

- Charlatans will try to take advantage of many aspects of the experience.

- There are those who will complain about how the matter is handled, and there will be some attempts to gain an advantage from doing that.

- In the end, the attempts made by the government to *fix it* will be largely ineffective.

- And, after all is said and done, more will be *said* than is *done*.

<u>Direction</u>

Here's how we will roll the book out:

- What is service?

- What does it mean to be a servant?

- How do we utilize the gifts we have?

- How do we decide where we will get involved?

- Is there a better way to do mission work?

- Is the outcome really that important?

- How do we deal with the lack of support in our projects?

- Is entrepreneurship the salvation of declining communities?

- What's next?

There are some Appendices included and referred to that will amplify particular parts of this book. They are excerpts, for the most part, from *Profit* and help to connect the ideas and recommendations presented there to this book.

At each stage, we will examine the components and factors that affect what we encounter. One of the things we see as a real impediment to success is a lack of <u>perseverance.</u> It seems that it is all too easy to just give up when the going gets a bit tough. Many seem to feel that we are just to go through the motions and let it go at that. After all, it is one thing to have people intellectually prepared, but it is quite another thing to have them <u>emotionally</u> prepared. Serving people can be a messy business, and not everyone is ready for the negativity that lies before them.

The challenge of this book is the struggle to recruit, train, motivate, and deploy *servants* out into the jungle of needy souls. There are those who will bail on the process before they are even ready to be deployed. Even more won't be up to the task once they get involved. These occurrences will certainly detract from the effort, but they must be dealt with in order to make any meaningful progress. However, unless one is just too faint-hearted to persevere, the experience can be very significant to growth as a human being.

The Challenge

As sort of a Commencement challenge, we will provide some particular places where readers might want to get involved, at least initially. We want to provide alternatives for those who aren't entrepreneurs themselves, or who want to *try something on for size*. We aren't talking about *run-of-the-mill* ideas or projects. Passion plays a very significant role. Trust us; without that, you will lose team members very quickly when the process gets difficult.

We also want to give you some tips on team building. Even if you aren't planning to be a leader, this type of organization calls for people who understand the why and can be great support cast members.

Additionally, we want to give some help with regard to moving forward with and, hopefully, after COVID-19. A lot is being learned that will impact how business is done in the future. We place this at the end because it is not possible to predict the future when we don't know what drastic changes are ahead of us. One of the necessary attributes of an entrepreneurial venture is: being *nimble*. Opportunities can appear and disappear very quickly, and we want to provide you with as much guidance as we can. There are ways to quickly adjust. We want to give you guidance for certain scenarios.

<u>Getting Started</u>

There is a Pakistani proverb that says: "If you are going to eat an elephant, you must start somewhere." This may be the most critical step as it can be the main direction that you will end up choosing. Our experience has shown that the best approach is to begin with the end in mind. By doing this, we can foresee some of the pitfalls that can wreck our project. Many people think (justifiably so, in many instances) that entrepreneurs are those people who get some notion that gets them all fired up, but they lose interest when the going gets a little tough. While the definition of an entrepreneur is *one who takes the risk*, you must have more going for you than *rolling the dice* on a project. For us, we don't consider ourselves to be risk-takers, pe rse. By most measures, Nathan is a visionary. That can certainly be risky, but not so much so if you are willing to do your homework, i.e., due diligence. Much will be written about that later as we consider which projects we take on.

Not everyone is going to get "all in," either. So, if we are careful when making the choices of participants, we can have a better chance of having the kind of outcome that we are looking for. As stated before, we can never expect things to go completely the way we want. Yet, if we lose too many of our team, we cannot expect to have the kind of outcome we seek. Nathan was fortunate for over 50 years to have a partner (wife) who was supportive but sometimes begrudgingly so. She came to realize that he liked a challenge, and she honored that to a point. He can remember her saying many times, "I just don't want to end up being a pauper!" He misses her support. Many really successful people had a foil to engage in dialogue that helped provide a crucible in which to grind out better plans.

It is our desire to use the experiences we have had to help others be enriched and prepared for the journey that they choose to undertake. Begin this with an open mind and a heart for what you are involved in. It is quite likely that you are going to be blessed beyond your imagination. Your attitude is what drives you, and it is important to have your heart in it.

Importance of Worldview

Many people don't even know what *worldview* is, and even those who do, don't think much about it. Merriam-Webster's definition is: a comprehensive conception or apprehension of the world, especially from a specific standpoint. More are aware of the concept of "paradigm". They are generally defined as a framework that has unwritten rules and directs actions. It is just a way of looking at the world, aka *worldview.* While some think of worldview as being in the conscious state of mind, others are convinced that this only manifests itself when it is triggered by a crisis of faith. It seems that, according to Webster's definition, standpoint is crucial to understanding the rub. Every one of the world's religions probably has a worldview, and they can approach the world from very different perspectives. For instance, the view of heaven will most likely determine how a person lives on earth. Some believe that martyring yourself for the faith gets you an immediate place. Most of the others don't share that view.

The point is: the colliding of differing viewpoints can be very dramatic. In our culture today, we don't find people giving up their point-of-view very readily. Part of the reason, as we can determine, has to do with the pervasiveness of the internet. Anyone can throw their point out in the cosmos, and nothing ever gets settled. The anonymity of this medium quite often allows people to avoid the consequences of their statements. Everyone's an expert. That goes for the media as well.

Rational-lies

Nathan has become convinced through observation and other sources that one of the most powerful words in our vocabulary is: rationalize. It is purposely spelled differently in the title of this section because we lie to ourselves all the time. The way in which we come to a decision about a situation that we encounter is to move through the rationalization process – upward or downward. Let's take an example of how this works:

> We see a person standing on a corner with a sign that says, "Will work for food". Our first reaction may be to ignore the person. If we make that decision, it is perhaps a cascading effect that quickly gets us there. For instance, we might think that the person just wants some money; they do not want food money. So we decide that they aren't really that bad off; they must want money to buy drugs. At that point, we quickly convinced ourselves that we were not going to be fooled by this person, and he/she would be better off if we didn't give him/her money.

Our guess is that most of us go through such a process. We may or may not be correct in our assessment of the situation, but we have *rationalized* that we are correct. Nathan actually was confronted by a rather well-dressed man in a shopping center parking lot once. He said he needed money for something. Nathan told him that a church nearby would probably help him. His reply was that he had tried that, and they wouldn't. Nathan hardly ever carries any cash, so he was off the hook. The man moved on to the next person.

This might seem simple enough, but charitable organizations deal with this all the time. It's just tough to determine the right course of action, but Philip Zimbardo has studied the matter of evil that good people do. Now, we are not saying that passing a panhandler is evil; but Zimbardo says that evil is the exercise of power. In other words, when we have the power to do something important and don't, that is evil. In Zimbardo's book, *the Lucifer Effect*, this is referred to as a *crime of opportunity*. Before you get upset by such an accusation, he also says that we typically go about dealing with such situations (or not) on an individual level. The problem lies with the *system*. This is the legal, political, economic, and cultural background.

When people fall prey to social mores or *the way the system works,* they need to be aware of the fallacy of wanting to *understand* the perpetrator. Zimbardo tells us that understanding is not an excuse. Each person is responsible for their own actions, and excusing them because the system is at fault is not the right answer.

We Need Heroes

Zimbardo describes a hero as someone who acts when others are passive and acts socio-centrically, not egocentrically. He goes on to say that most people are guilty of the evil of inaction because we have been told to not get involved. In our culture, the ones considered heroes are the exceptions; they have supernatural talents. However, most heroes are actually ordinary people. It is a heroic act.

Daniel Goleman says that we aren't more compassionate because we are focused in the wrong direction. If we self-focus, we tend to miss what is going on around us. We don't notice because we don't act. The new thinking about compassion from social neuroscience is that our default wiring is to help others in need. When we do help them, we tend to empathize.

In their book, *Hero-makers*, Dave Ferguson and Warren Bird spell out a plan to transfer our *heroism* in a multiplier effect. The challenge is to recruit them first. That step of *character development* is not clear, but it is vitally important. That's really what this book is about: recruiting people that are willing and able to be appropriately sensitized to the needs of those they seek to serve, train, and deploy them. We are really focusing on the recruiting aspect, so we will put together the steps necessary to accomplish that process.

Acting Socio-centrically

Have you ever heard the difference between involvement and commitment? Consider a breakfast of bacon and eggs. The chicken was involved, but the pig was committed – albeit reluctantly, no doubt. We have a lot of people involved in service, but how many of them are also committed? In other words, are we just putting bandages on gaping wounds, or are we working on cleaning up thorny paths so they never happen? Nathan's book, *The Dignity of Profit,* is subtitled, *Creating Community through Entrepreneurship.* To our way of thinking, Robert Lupton has made a powerful case for using this sociocentric methodology to help reduce poverty in a powerful way. *Profit* described the call that we have as Christians to go out into the field to make a difference and the landscape that awaits those servants who do. A general approach to the way this plays out at the field level was provided, but now, there is some actual experience that we can use to flesh out the process.

Neither of us really thought much of *social entrepreneurship* until we had a chance to see how it could work to help change lives and improve local economies. Many non-profit organizations shy away from helping for-profit businesses. The exception has been grants and lending in economicallydepressed areas. However, without proper guidance, this is largely ineffective. Some very innovative approaches are now available to those who want to be successful.

Mahatma Gandhi once said: "You must be the change that you wish to see in the world." We hope that you are reading this book because you believe you can make a difference.

Putting This into Focus

As we begin this challenging task, we need to consider how we can keep a clear focus on our planning. At the core is the need for *leadership*. This squares with the notion of *Hero-makers.* Creating leaders is the business of those who have become heroes and now need to re-create themselves (sort of). We are not going to try to relate all of the aspects of that book, but we can lay out how this works in practice.

Creating *community* means that we follow the plan to bring people together in a group that is equipped to function effectively. The giftedness of the members has to mesh together to deal with their respective challenges. In doing so and beginning to function as a group, new leaders will be drawn in. The need is for new groups to arise out of the original ones. Replication will not only make the original project(s) more effective, but it will allow the lessons learned to be utilized over and over. OK, call it multi-level marketing if you wish; but thinking and acting socio-centrically places the true focus on needs other than our own.

Our experience with projects that involve churches and other benevolent organizations is that it is often difficult to keep the proper focus. Leadership is critical to being able to *stay the course*. You'll hear that again, but it is often quite easy to get discouraged. With motivation being one of the major tasks of leaders, making sure that adequate leadership is part of the equation is vital to success. Hopefully, we can convey the need for service and leadership to walk hand-in-hand. They are not designed to be exclusive of one another.

"Do you live expectantly? Do the little things excite you? Do you imagine the improbable and expect the impossible? Life is full and running over with opportunities to see God's hand in little things. Only the most sensitive of His servants see them, smile, and live on tiptoe." Chuck Swindoll

CHAPTER 1

Service: The Key to Success

"You may be an ambassador to England or France.
You may like to gamble, you might like to dance.
You may be the heavyweight champion of the world.
You may be a socialite with a long string of pearls.

But you're gonna have to serve somebody, yes.
Indeed, you're gonna have to serve somebody.
Well, it may be the devil, or it may be the Lord.
But you're gonna have to serve somebody..."

Bob Dylan

When faced with determining what something really is – like service – it might be helpful to go to a good dictionary to get the *official* meaning. Admittedly, this came from a member of a Sunday School class, where Nathan was a member, who would always ask: "What does the dictionary say this means?" I finally got it and looked up the meaning before I embarked on my presentation. It really is a good idea, don't you think? After all, it doesn't make much sense to not clear the air before you start.

All that being said, some of the definitions we found seemed to be rather negative. Maybe it was because we were looking the word up online, and perhaps it was a function of how people have searched for it. The best one says that it is the *action of helping or doing work for someone.* Synonyms include: · *good turn · favor · kindness · helping hand · assistance · help · aid · offices · ministrations.* The ones that seemed negative generally had to do with manual labor and/or working as a servant. We'll talk a bit more about the servant aspect later, but consider that we are referring here to those things that make life better for the one for whom the *service* is intended.

The term *good turn* is not used that much these days. The Boy Scouts used to ask the boys to *do a good turn daily*. There's a story about a Scoutmaster who sent his troop out to do a good turn at one meeting. When one group of them came back, he asked the first boy what his deed was, and the boy replied: "I helped an old lady across the street." One-by-one, the next five boys said that they did the same as the first boy. The Scoutmaster thought that was odd, so he asked them why they all did the same deed. They replied that the old lady didn't want to go!

Service businesses seem to do pretty well these days, especially considering that we generally don't import them from China or wherever. We do have a lot of people coming from other countries, however, that perform services for us. That has been going on for a long time. There are lots of references in the Bible regarding foreigners working somewhere, and many times, they were slaves or indentured servants. That's not the same, though. I mean, we don't have mechanics that work in the *Service Department* of a car dealership who are considered slaves or servants do we? Last time we checked, those folks did quite well financially. Their lifestyle may not be that of a whitecollar worker, but we all are slaves to something.

OK, so this might be missing the point a bit; but where we are trying to lead readers is into a consideration of what service really means when it is not a paid gig. Employees in a *social service* organization may be in paid positions, but there are lots of people who do social work that do it out of a desire to be of *service* to their fellow humans. So, the point is not to get too worked up over the narrowness of the definition. What we need to consider is how we serve others in a way that helps to lift them up rather than putting them down. That's where the matter of *dignity* comes into play.

Consider, if you will, these ways that can be considered components of service:

Authenticity,   *credibility,*   *sincerity,*   *responsibility,*

perseverance,   *objectivity,*   *passion,*

Vision,   *humility,*   *creativity,*   *reliability,*   *concern,*

compassion,   *empathy,*   *integrity.*

It just seems to us that it is pretty hard to be effective at serving others without at least a fair dose of all of these virtues. Perhaps the primary reason is that it is human nature to gravitate to the things we feel comfortable doing. You can probably see how that might be a problem if you are lacking sufficient gifting in most of the items in the first row.

Here are some ways that we can serve others. Some of these are areas that require major training or skills. Some of them don't, but the less demanding ones can be a gateway for you or those that you could refer them to get exactly what they need:

health care, construction, education, social service, emotional support, food distribution, financial assistance, workforce development, career training, entrepreneurship, cleanup of property, forest service, child care, automotive care/repair, technical training, job placement, aiding the homeless, veteran's assistance.

Where Do Christians Fit into This?

There was an interesting exchange in Mark 10 between Jesus and two disciples who were brothers. They wanted a position of authority, but Jesus took the conversation off in a different direction. They were taken down a few notches when He told them that "whoever wants to become great among you must be your servant, and whoever wants to be first must be slave of all. For even the Son of Man did not come to be served, but to serve..." **(vv. 43b-45a)** Alistar Begg says that the church has struggled with a false notion: "One of the great lies that exist in almost every generation is the idea that the more the people of God look like, sound like, act like, live like those who are not the people of God, the better able God's people then will be able to reach their generation." He goes on to say, "What we discover in this passage is that the measure of an individual's greatness is not in the number of servants in their house, but the extent to which that individual is willing to live in the service of others."

The church's mission is to serve the world by sharing the love God gives. The church's service is to offer hospitality to the lonely and the stranger. The church is not a club with closed membership but a house where the door is always open, and there is always a place for hungry souls at the table **(Matt. 25: 31-42)**. The church's service is to offer God's healing to the sick in body, mind, spirit, and relationship; to extend Christ's outreach to those who live "having no hope and without God" **(Eph. 2:12)**; to seek to erase the lines that divide people; to bear witness to the truth and be the conscience of society.

Natural Church Development (NCD) is a world-wide program that includes over 80,000 churches in many different denominations. The basic modality of this program involves an assessment that covers eight *quality characteristics*. The goal of a church that takes on this program is to have a composite score in these areas that correlates with the scores of *healthy churches*. One of the quality characteristics that deal with service is *need-oriented evangelism*. That concept won Nathan over due to its focusing on filling a need. While this is primarily considered a good way to be successful as an entrepreneur, it is also good advice for the church. After all, we are the ones who have the best answer to solve the most pressing needs we face in our society: Jesus Christ.

Our experience has shown us that many Christians want to share the gospel with a needy world. Unfortunately, the initial contact they have is with folks that are near to where they live. In most rural areas, the challenge is very great. Since they have a relatively small circle of friends and acquaintances that they interact with, there isn't a lot of opportunity to reach people on the deep levels that evangelism demands. Some of them try to reach out to friends and family, but this isn't usually very productive. People develop paradigms over time, and new information may not be welcome. Additionally, the people who are inclined to consider a Christian lifestyle may already be involved in a church (or at least use that as an excuse to ward off those who engage in some type of evangelism).

Speaking of the church's need to be involved in such activities, it seems that many churches are just too inwardly focused to recognize the importance of reaching out to the very people that need to hear the *good news.* Some of these people may be very involved in *church work –* those necessary activities that help keep the church running smoothly. However, the real *work of the church* mostly lies outside the walls of the church building. It is not our purview to engage in trying to solve all the church's problems, but it is important to recognize that we need to be *in the world* as the Apostle Paul encouraged us to be. After all, the Great Commission calls us to go into the world and to make disciples. This doesn't mean that it is not important and honorable to fold the worship bulletins on Friday afternoons or be an usher at church services. Even those activities have the capacity to be evangelical.

It is important to note that *evangelism* is something that is best left to those who have that gift. On the other hand, Christian Schwarz, the creator of NCD, notes that we are called to be *evangelical.* Being evangelical means that we believe in a *born-again* experience as the way of salvation and in the authority of the Scripture as God's revelation to humanity. It is these items that lead us to spread the Gospel. We can and should all do that. To that end, we can be very true to the calling we have when we seek to reach people where they are most needy – thus the need-oriented approach.

One of the major purposes of this book is to help prepare Christians to feel more comfortable in sharing their faith while actually performing some act of kindness or hospitality to those who are in the darkness of absence from Christ. It might seem that we are looking to criticize those who are working in churches in either paid or unpaid positions. That's certainly not our purpose, but many churches (especially larger ones) have become very bureaucratic and hierarchal, thus missing the crying need for those who are lost.

Chuck Swindoll writes: "In our culture—our schools, our offices and factories, our lunchrooms and boardrooms, our halls of ivy and our halls of justice—we need men and women of God, including young people of God. We need respected professionals, athletes, homemakers, teachers, public figures, and private citizens who will promote the things of God, who will stand alone—stand tall, stand firm, stand strong!" **(Swindoll, 2020)**

<u>Meaningful Service</u>

We touched a bit in earlier comments about ways to be in service. It might be well to veer off the path a little to try to get to the heart of the matter. Nathan speaks of the times when he was on a mission trip or housing rehab program, where volunteers shared how good it made them feel to do something for someone else. He would be the first one to say that feeling good about yourself and your actions is a good thing. Surely, God rewards us with a rush of self-adulation in times like that. It is important to note that much time, study, research, and experience was spent in his writing *The Dignity of Profit*. In that book, there were many instances of doing the wrong thing for the right reasons. Dignity is denied to people who are recipients of the service of others when that service misses the mark. Let us share one example that Robert Lupton (Charity Detox) cited, which was well-intended.

It seems that John Coors, former leader of America's largest brewing operation, had become quite successful at creating very innovative means of solving challenging problems. One he called the Circle of Light, took on the task of lighting subSaharan Africa where there was no electricity to power traditional means. It was going to address a whole spectrum of serious environmental, health, and social issues. This was a massive project that used propane tanks and batteries to provide sources for cooking and lighting. Sadly, the project failed because the government didn't have the resources to keep it going; therefore, the farmers that were the intended beneficiaries of the project went back to using the money to produce their crops. Coors bailed on the project, but he found a better way to help the people with for-profit enterprises and local involvement.

"It's a tragedy when nonprofits—with all the best intentions—end up actually making things worse for the communities they serve." This was shared by Amira Diamond and Melinda Kramer in a March 2019 article about community development. The gist of the article was that ignoring the people that we intend to help can actually lead us (and them) off in the wrong direction.

Lupton shares many stories about success and failure. One thing he was asked at the seminar he held in St. Louis had to do with the need to involve business people in the process. He elaborates extensively about this in *Charity Detox*. He also writes about social entrepreneurs and how the partnership between nonprofits and for-profits is a powerful concept. Let us share a bit about how that works.

Social Entrepreneurship – A Relatively New Concept

It was mentioned earlier that we are fairly new recruits to the *social entrepreneurship* concept. As in John Coors' experience, the loss of the profit motive can lead to all types of undesirable outcomes. Nathan expressed this extensively in *Profit*, for he was particularly leery of many of the folks that were trying to make a successful endeavor out of a non- profit idea. The tipping point was the need to get unencumbered capital focused on any real outcome scenario. Coors was so jaundiced from his first experience that he just didn't feel that non-profits were even a potential solution.

Certainly, there is a lot of truth to that, but there has to be the desire to do something truly socially-conscious regardless of which path you take. If you turn over a large portion of the major source of materials to a single entity, for instance, you run the risk of a monopoly that may drive costs out of the acceptable range for profitability. At that point, the single source could become the driver of the entire industry. OK, I know that monopolies are hard to pull off these days, but there are still instances where this happens on a small scale. China essentially took over the rare earth minerals market several years ago. When you have a situation like that, there could be a couple of avenues to consider. As prices reach extreme levels, a few larger manufacturers could put pressure on the source to force them to be more willing to work with the producers. Alternatively (and perhaps simultaneously), manufacturers may aggressively seek lower-cost substitutes or look for a new methodology in order to streamline operations. These are certainly short-sighted vendors, but many are not in it for the long haul anyway.

Social Consciousness as a Component of Service

Social consciousness may be a fickle dance partner in many ways. Back when the notion of *going green* came along, manufacturers jumped on the bandwagon and raised prices in this new way to make themselves feel good while helping the bottom line. Many of the new, environmentally sensitive products and services were just window-dressing. We may appear to be turning a blind eye to the situation if we don't buy into the *new way of doing things*. Nathan taught an on-line college business ethics course once, and it offered case studies designed to show real-world experiences to consider. Some were fairly obvious, but others were a bit challenging. A particular example was about a factory in rural Idaho that had been cited for excessive polluting. Through some of their efforts, the company reduced the levels by approximately 25 %. The total employment was about 70 people, but that was a big number for the small town where the factory was located. He was surprised at many of the students' lack of concern for the number of people that would be laid off if the factory closed down. Realistically, the total population of the town was not particularly affected by the emissions, and the impact seemed to be more related to the loss of jobs anyway. Most of the students didn't seem to get it.

The point is: just about all of life is a matter of *trade-offs*. When you get up in the morning, you have made a decision to go about the day's activities rather than go for a few more zzzzs. Some choose to try to get a jump on the day, but others take a little longer to take it on. A choice to be overly interested in our environment is a popular one today, and there is certainly a case to be made for some of the actions that are taken in the name of *saving the planet*. Personally, we tend to look to God to lead us in our thinking and choices in such matters, but that doesn't mean that we don't care. Pollution is a disgusting thing and takes away from the beauty of God's creation. However, sometimes the trade-off is, unfortunately a drain on the financial resources that are going to have to be thrown at the problem.

The best choice here is the same as most situations that have to be dealt with: just do the right thing in the first place. Nathan's dad used to say that if you throw trash on the ground or whatever, you should pick it up.

If that is the case, perhaps you will be more careful about where you put your trash. Frankly, we just can't take on all the issues; we have to make trade-offs. On the other hand, from a social concern perspective, we can look at how we can help people create something to be environmentally sensitive to the point that they are able to. Then, people who can and will take on doing some of the cleanup that is left to be done, become the heroes of that story.

It just makes sense that we all engage in socially responsible activities, but we can, at the same time, also be sensitive to the efforts the producers are undertaking to meet the demands of the population at large. Ludwig von Mises (pp. 1-8) points out that we have mass merchants, shopping malls, etc., because the consumer demands them. People who seek to destroy what has been created do so at their own peril. Business people get blamed for not being sensitive to the consumer wants and needs. Yet, they don't understand what a challenge that is. Especially in the 21st century, we are seeing a major shift in the way we deliver goods and services. This is probably a direct result of some entrepreneur trying to get one up on the competition. After all, that's how we survive and hopefully thrive, isn't it?

On the other hand, compassion is a powerful force for good, for the most part. The problem arises when we leave God out of consideration. There were several responses to a blog entitled, *Why Is It Important to Care about Others?* Many of the comments were on target, except that they referred to *nature* and *honoring our history.* Of course, these are important factors; but they have no real substance to them. Our Creator provided these and other components of our universe, and considering them as some sort of entity of their own misses the mark entirely. Certainly, making the matter all about yourself is pretty egotistical as well.

Entrepreneurs Nonetheless

Entrepreneurs *take the risk.* The only difference between for profit entrepreneurs and non-profit ones is that the risk is handled differently. Depending on how a non-profit is structured, the demise of the operation could be laid on the non-profit the same way it is with a for-profit. Those who provide grants to nonprofits have become more conscious of the pitfalls that might await them. Someone is held responsible with little or no recourse. Admittedly, it is a bit more complicated than that. The terms of the grant will dictate a lot, but generally, most grantors have been burned before and don't wish to have that happen again.

This just points to the necessity of taking good care to understand what you are getting into. The story of John Coors underscores the problems that may be out there lurking in wait for unsuspecting souls. Nathan found himself in a mess in a non-profit venture that was due to some issues regarding a possible conflict of interest. While such matters do exist with for-profits, the likelihood there is much less. He would have avoided it if there hadn't been some compelling need to get funding from sources that only made grants to nonprofits.

The entrepreneurial spirit that is necessary in many start-up ventures is not the exclusive province of the for-profit ones. Laurie Beth Jones calls people who create start-ups in the religious context: *spiritreneurs*. This tends to be more of the concept that some have regarding *social entrepreneurs*. That is, charitable organizations "that follow solid business plans and create earning streams that sustain the non-profit work." There is more on that to come later, but the point to make is: there is room for both methods if there is a desire to create wealth. Accountability needs to be a part of either way.

True innovation will make it through the gauntlet to success if it meets the needs and desires of the consuming public. We live in a world where we are constantly barraged by sellers hawking the newest and most exciting products and services. Additionally, we have some radically new ways to deliver these to the ultimate consumer. Amazon has changed the retail landscape, and we have yet to see the outcome. The company has become so pervasive that we are hardly able to digest the innovation before something even newer comes along. You have to feel sorry for those of us who always have to have the newest and most exciting items available. Oh, and don't forget about price drops, which mean you paid a much larger sum just a short time ago.

Tom Peters, in *A Passion for Excellence*, told of a group in the 3M organization that was known as: *Skunkworks*. They had an autonomous operation and were free to be as creative as they wanted to be. This concept has been used in other innovationoriented organizations, and it has proved to be very effective in many cases. Larry Wilson described in *Changing the Game, A New Way of Selling* how Ford Motor Company radically departed from the normal way innovation is practiced in the automobile industry. When the Taurus was developed, the designers went to customers to get input from the end-users. This departure from tradition made the Taurus very successful. Imagine how it must felt to have been one of those who participated in designing the car.

Whether it is a non-profit or a for-profit concept, an entrepreneurial spirit is called for. Laurie Beth Jones put it this way: "Spiritreneurs are curious about everything – they stay fascinated watching a process unfold rather than fearing the end results." It's truly hard to go after something great if you are always concerned that you will not be successful. If God is in what you are doing, the outcome will be what He wants as long as you stay faithful.

What Does this Mean for Us?

It may seem that we have wandered a bit far off track here, but we can only be of *service* to others if we address their challenges appropriately. If we are talking about consumers, we are looking more at the *end game*. However, if we are working with producers, we must deal with market issues as well. Inherent in that arena is the problem of seemingly constant change. It's not just innovation with respect to the product/service itself. Equipment, supply channels, employer/employee matters, environmental concerns, legal issues…the list seemingly goes on and on.

As we look at how we can be of service to entrepreneurs and their intended *customers*, we need to know a few things. Why are we doing this? What do we want to accomplish? What kind of service are we seeking to provide? What do we need to know before we embark on our journey to help them? What do we need to have in order to take on the task at hand? How do we handle the challenges that arise? How do we measure success?

"To me, it is important to understand that service doesn't cost, it pays. When we are unwilling to give of ourselves and our material possessions, it is not just selfishness that is involved. We assume that we are giving and not getting anything in return." **Cynthia Tobias**

CHAPTER 2

What Does It Mean to Be a Servant?

"….a servant doesn't care who gets the glory. Remember that. A servant has one great goal, and that is to make the person he serves look better, to make that person even more successful. A servant does not want the person he serves to fail. A servant doesn't care who thinks what, just so the job gets done." **Chuck Swindoll**

Here are a few definitions of a servant. It's interesting how broad the range is between some of these:

1. A person who performs duties for others, especially a person employed in a house on domestic duties or as a personal attendant.

2. A person employed in the service of a government

3. A devoted and helpful follower or supporter – a tireless servant of God.

4. One that serves others, a public servant especially: one that performs duties about the person or home of a master or personal employer

5. A person who maintains and supports but doesn't produce anything.

The last one in this list seems rather negative. In the Bible, being God's servant is an honorable position. Throughout the New Testament, the word bondservant or servant is applied to someone who is absolutely devoted to Jesus.

When we look at servant leadership, we find the following characteristics. These are certainly more positive:

Empathy,   *listening,*   *awareness,*   *healing,*

conceptualization,   *persuasive,*

Stewardship,   *foresight,*   *community building ,*   *committed,*

to the growth of others.

Understanding Servanthood

It's interesting that most of our pictures of being a *servant* aren't particularly admirable. As recent as the 1950s and even later, many households had what was known as *domestic servants.* For well-to-do families, these positions were more than just lower-class jobs. Factory work and the minimum wage helped to change the landscape as it relates to this type of job. Only the very wealthy of today have servants of this type on staff. Catering companies have workers who perform these duties for occasions, but they are normally considered servants. Our lexicon has changed over the years since the 50s, so that we now have begun to see servanthood in a different light.

The project that Nathan helped to launch was designed for several purposes. It is a small business incubator – shared locations for entrepreneurs to start or expand their businesses. It is also a community center of sorts for meetings, etc. The most visible part is a café that functions to help support the operational costs of the entire facility, but it is primarily a training center for people who need to learn some life skills and customer service procedures. In any retail situation, there is a crying need for workers who are *really* serving their customers. With the digital age in full swing, face-to-face encounters mean a lot to people who really need support that is hard to access online. As the population as a whole grows older, many of those who expect good service will not be as prevalent as in times past. This means opportunities, but it also brings loss to others. Shopping online is appealing to more and more people as our culture embraces the easy access to computers and smartphones. However, shopping on-line can be very frustrating when you need *customer service.*

Perhaps we need to find a new way to serve people. There's no way any of these digital devices will go away, but have you used the ordering kiosk at McDonald's? Heck, the café mentioned above has a terrible time keeping the internet up to process credit and debit transactions. No one has any time these days, but the old saying, "Haste makes waste," still applies. Amazon pushes the envelope in many ways, but getting into delivery is going to be tough on a lot of businesses. It's all about how to outdo the competition. There are different jobs being created, and some are going unfilled.

There was a bank in St. Charles, Missouri, that helped pioneer a new concept in the drive-through portion of handling customer transactions on-site. The tellers who operated that part of the process were not seen in person by the customers. Neither were most transactions inside the bank. The stations were like ATMs with video interchange between customers and tellers. It seemed to work pretty well, but it doesn't seem to catch on in many areas. It may be that the cost of changing over is too high and relegated to new installations, and there haven't been that many new installations – just name changes. There are transactions that have to be done inside the bank, but there is a receptionist that does that. This may not be a revolution in customer service, but it is certainly more personal than doing it on-line or talking to someone on the phone when you can't see their non-verbal communication.

There was a time around the stock market crash in 2007-08 when merchants and other service people became a lot more pleasant. At that time, customers were surly a lot of the time.

It's pretty easy to understand: salespeople needed the business, but customers didn't have the money. Frustration for all! Jobs that depended on customers/clients feeling satisfied were staffed by workers who knew the value of a happy customer. The irony is that the government is still taking care of so many people that many jobs go unfilled when there are actually able people who aren't interested in working. Rural areas that provide services that everyone needs – food, medicine, housing, gasoline, etc. – do OK with those on some sort of financial assistance. However, the middle class is almost non-existent. Businesses are having a tough time finding people to serve. Trying to get entrepreneurs interested in setting up shop is a challenging situation.

In *The Dignity of Profit*, Nathan often cited from a couple of books: *The Coming Jobs War* by James Clifton and The Great Equalizer by David Smick. Clifton paints a grim picture about how China and India are gaining on the U.S. in having people actually working. Smick points out that the control of our economy is in the hands of a few players, and he encourages communities to take charge of their situation. He promotes the idea of entrepreneurship, and he calls the solution: Main Street Capitalism. However, he also encourages cities and towns to get youth involved earlier. Getting people together to address the situation is extremely important. We all have a stake in this, and socialism is not the answer. We can't just look to others to take care of us, and it is vitally important that we care about one another.

Servanthood as the Catalyst

You may be thinking that *servanthood* can't really be the answer, can it? Bear with us a little bit, and perhaps you will see what we are getting at. From the perspective of a manager, just doing your job can be awfully appealing. We have had lots of jobs that are manager- or leadership-level positions. The rarified air of a lofty level of responsibility can get very lonely, and it can be an easy target. Nathan learned in the military that the senior officer is usually the one who gets canned if things go wrong. We see that quite often in sports. In both cases, if you get the chance to fire all of the assistants and keep your job, you must have a mutiny or have something on the owner of the team. The service that the lower-level *managers* provide is invaluable in making sure things go as designed. You have to suffer some abuse in many cases, but you then have the option of putting up with it or moving on. Everyone has to do their part, but it is easy to feel that the people in charge must have been smoking something funny to make the decisions that they made in certain situations.

Nathan tells a story he heard once about a very successful football coach who faced a difficult situation with just a few seconds left in the game. All the team needed to do was to hold on and make a first down to be able to run out the clock. His team had the ball on their own forty- yard-line and a three-point lead when his first-team quarterback left the game with an injury. The backup quarterback went in and was injured on the first play. There was no regular quarterback left, so the coach decided to put in the punter. The punter was also a running back, so the coach gave him some simple instructions: run the ball on the first play that he was in, then punt the ball into the end zone. The punter went and received the ball from the center and ran the ball all the way down to the one-yard-line. Then he punted the ball into the end zone as directed. Fortunately for the team (and the punter), the buzzer sounded to end the game just as the ball crossed into the end zone, and victory was secured. As everyone on the winning side jumped, shouted, and cheered, the coach asked the punter what in the world was he thinking when he kicked the ball. The punter very frankly responded: "I was remarking to myself that we must have the dumbest coach in the league!"

Sometimes, it is important to understand the big picture when you have agreed to serve. If you are a volunteer, you may not care to know a lot about the reason this task is important. To us though, when we are asked or volunteer to serve in a certain capacity, considering the purpose of the activity should be important. We wrote earlier that a *good feeling*, while desirable, is not the primary reason for service. If we take on *servanthood*, we don't want to end up like the punter – blindly doing a specific task without considering the potential outcome. If we find ourselves in a position of authority, our servanthood takes on a different responsibility. Not only are we responsible to the one/s we serve as one in charge of a group or a task, we are responsible to those who are serving under us.

As mentioned above, military leaders must ensure that the task is done correctly and effectively, and they must also guide their subordinates in order to prepare them for their responsibilities. This includes safety and other aspects of their wellbeing. Military leaders, who don't have the respect of those under their charge, may find themselves in serious trouble when things go wrong if they haven't served well.

Servanthood as a Profession

Considering *servanthood* to be a profession requires a bit of change in the way we think about *leadership*. According to Wikipedia, being a servant leader is "different from traditional leadership where the leader's main focus is the thriving of their company or organizations. A Servant

Leader shares power, puts the needs of the employees first, and helps people develop and perform as highly as possible. It inverts the norm, which puts the customer service associates as a main priority. Instead of the people working to serve the leader, the leader exists to serve the people."

When Rehoboam was made king of Israel, he was told: "If you will be a servant to this people, be considerate of their needs and respond with compassion, work things out with them, they'll end up doing anything for you." He refused to heed this advice and God's judgment was exacted on him. A major part of Rehoboam's downfall started with his seeking the wrong counsel. Seeking Godly counsel is critical in being able to succeed as a leader. The story of Rehoboam brings that point home very dramatically. **(1 Kings 12: 7 –19 MSG)**

The phrase *servant leadership* was first popularized by Robert K. Greenleaf in an essay published in 1970. It was not the first time that the notion was put forth. King Frederick II of Prussia (1740 – 1786) famously portrayed himself as the "first servant of the state". It's not clear whether he really was, but it does show that authoritarian rule was challenged to some degree. Our view is that while *authoritarianism* may be less prevalent in many places, it has not necessarily become that way in favor of *servant leadership*. Juan Peron of Argentina sought to please his constituents in order to get away with whatever he wanted to. The failure of his regime is testimony of his missing the mark.

Ken Blanchard, Author of *The One Minute Manager*, put it like this:

"The only way I have seen organizations get great results and great human satisfaction is when people understand the power of servant leadership. You know, unfortunately over 50% of the workforce in our country are disengaged. Their excitement is after work, rather than in work. And it doesn't have to be that way, because people are spending a majority of their days at work. And how can we create a culture and a work environment that excites people? Because we've seen what self-serving leaders have done. They've demotivated people. They've caused major negative problems in government, every sector of society all around the world, and we can make a difference. The only way to get great results and great human satisfaction is with servant leadership."

Being a *servant leader* is not really a profession unless you consider *human resources managers* as being so. Not many of them are focused on the employees, but they should be. In many ways, they are considered assets, but leaders tend to view them differently. It seems that part of that attitude has come from the advent of labor unions. Some workers have demands for working conditions and the like, but most of the demands seem to focus on money, vacations, etc. There has been an adversarial situation in many industries, and it doesn't seem to be getting better.

Another thing that seems to militate against *serving* your employees is that many will take advantage of it. That has happened to most managers. "Give them an inch, and they take a mile." This is where *relationships* come into play. We hear of companies that give big bonuses or some other reward to their employees, but most of the time the effect is the desired one if the employees are being rewarded for doing something other than their regular requirements. The reward also has to be timely and truly deserved.

Nonetheless, there are some aspects of being a servant leader that doesn't require all of the politics that get involved in the scenarios cited above. For instance, helping employees do their job better is a great service to them and the company. Doing so doesn't require any major effort or expenditure in many cases. Even so, the expenditure may be something that the owner or manager would rather not have to make. However, if it makes sense and benefits the employee in important ways, it should probably be done if at all possible.

Social Entrepreneurship and Servant Leadership

What this means in this instance is that *social entrepreneurship* requires *servant leadership* to a high degree. We will discuss other forms of business activity in chapter 9, and they require servant leadership as well. So much of the exchange between parties in such ventures can become rather contentious. Maybe adversarial is a better term, but it shouldn't have to be that way. By its very nature, this type of enterprise is designed to be of major help (service) to the prospects. Obviously, we can't do it for them, but they have to feel that we are acting in their best interest. There are a lot of reasons that folks don't trust people who are trying to *help* them. Many of them are valid, but we will never get anywhere if we can't break through the tough veneer. Admittedly, most people who seek help really just want money. However, giving money to someone who is not prepared to use it appropriately is like giving red meat to a hungry animal and expecting him to listen to a message on its dietary habits.

One of the ways that we have sought to cut through this is to seek people who have an idea for a business but don't have a clue about creating a business plan. They need someone to *serve* them by walking them through the steps. However, even then, they want someone else to do it for them. There is a lot of mistrust as well. You can give some of these people a *non-disclosure agreement*, even if that doesn't suit them. They are just afraid that their wonderful idea is going to be stolen. Nathan worked with a lot of businesses as a broker, trying to help them sell their business. There are many instances when the seller has been upended by the buyer (and sometimes the broker). The problem is that without guidance, most of these people don't stand a chance. There are a lot of sharks out there.

While a lot of this paints a dim picture of the servant leader's lot, we hope to provide enough strength to the concept that you will want to give it your best effort. It is worth it for sure if you are doing God's work. Both of us can attest to it. We believe that Michael Slaughter sums it up in his book, *Change the World*. He says that volunteers serve at their convenience, but servants serve at their *inconvenience*.

Katie Delp of FCS Ministries (Robert Lupton's organization) shared this about their experience in neighborhoods in Atlanta:

> *"When we seek justice and equity for one group of people, we end up benefiting everyone. It's embedded in God's design for the world. When we seek first to live in the right relationship with each other, we find out that our flourishing really was bound up in each other's well being. We find these revelations delightful and encouraging. They may look like unexpected benefits, but we're reminded that they're part of the design."*

CHAPTER 3

How Does Servanthood Fit Our Purpose?

"The purpose of apple trees is not to produce apples; it is to produce more apple trees."
Christian Schwarz

Blaise Pascal (Pascal 1669) has been credited with the notion of a "God-shaped hole" in our hearts that only God can fill. This suggests it is the condition we find ourselves in when we have strayed away from God. A lot of what makes us restless is that we are here for a purpose, but we haven't determined what it is.

It helps to understand what your purpose in life is. You may already be there, so if you are, bear with us while we help those who are not sure about it. However, it would probably be helpful to go through all of this. Much of what is said in this chapter is done to help readers get pointed in the right direction. We love the saying: "One of the most disappointing things in life is when you reach the top of the ladder you have been climbing only to learn that the ladder was leaning against the wrong building." We have both been there, so we feel that helping others avoid this as much as possible is a good thing. It should also help to determine the outcome in positive ways.

Ever since Nathan became aware of the notion of *spiritual gifts*, he sought guidance from the Bible. There are several references to gifts – mainly from the apostle Paul. Being the do-it-yourself (DIY) person that he is, discerning his gifts was a process of reading Scripture and listening to various speakers, mainly people like Dr. Charles Stanley and others. While this can be helpful, we are not usually the best judge of ourselves. *Rationalization* was referred to earlier, and it can very easily be the way we determine such things. After all, if we like doing something, God surely means that we should use that to the best advantage. Well, while that is true to some extent, liking to spend time on a smartphone is perhaps not usually the best way to find our spiritual gifts. These devices are helping to destroy communities and relationships in many ways. As powerful as they are to make our lives more productive, keeping us from communicating so we can learn more about why we and others are here has to be something that we cannot welcome.

In his book, *Cure for the Common Life*, Max Lucado tells us that you are the on "you" there is. God made you that way. He would never ask you to be other than the way He made you. When you figure it out, you will have unleashed your passion.

Discovering Our Spiritual Gifts

Most theologians that we know believe that we all have gifts from God. Furthermore, we are expected to use these gifts to the glory of God. We will provide one listing of gifts later, but realize that gifts are not the same as talents. An athlete with great talent may not have a means of transferring that talent into a spiritual gift. You can argue the point, certainly, but being a professional athlete doesn't translate to Christian witnessing, on its face. Kurt Warner, Super Bowl-winning quarterback with the St. Louis Rams, would gather most of the team around him to pray before a game. There was a lot of controversy by some who contended that he was just doing it for notoriety. This sort of thing happens all the time, and those who kneel during the national anthem feel that they will use the spotlight the same as those who use it in other ways. Anyway, it wasn't the gift of athletic talent that directly gave them a connection with fans or impressionable children. It was the celebrity status that they had attained.

Christian Schwarz is the author of the Natural Church Development (NCD) program and many books dealing with the various facets of the program. The core of NCD is a group of eight building blocks that comprise the pathway to a healthy church. This is a program that now has included over 80,000 churches worldwide. By the use of an assessment tool (survey), churches can be compared to healthy churches. From their starting point in each of the eight building blocks, implementation of the NCD program should help lead them to become a healthy church, assuming that they are not already there. The prescription for the individual church is to work on the *lowest factor*, which is one of the building blocks. Once that has been chosen there are steps that can be taken to raise it to the 65% percentile level of that of the healthy churches in the program. We will be referring to NCD in different ways as we move forward. Specifically, *gift-based ministry* is the starting point for implementation, and determining one's spiritual gifts is extremely important as a person sets out to be effective in ministry.

We will not be delving deeply into this particular method of determining one's spiritual gift, but you may find that there is a way that you feel more comfortable with it. Go for it. In his book, *The 3 Colors of Ministry*, Schwarz points out that God intends to use our spiritual gifts to bring us joy (p. 59). However, we have each said – as have many others – that something we have been asked to do is "just not my gift". While that may actually be true, we have found that being exposed to new areas can open doors to new ministry opportunities, thereby launching a whole new adventure for us – with amazing joy. We have found a good spiritual gift assessment to be one of the most liberating things one can do. On the other hand, some find it to be disappointing due their lack of appreciation for what is going on. Gifts will change over time as we develop those latent values into the gifts that have been waiting for God's timing.

SPOILER ALERT!!! Criticism and complaining are not Spiritual Gifts.

Getting Directed into Ministry

If we are to live out the purpose that God has for us, we need to determine how we can be most effective in ministry. This doesn't mean that everyone should just go out and start something new. On the other hand, finding the thing that fits for you can be the way the door is opened to live out your purpose. Schwarz addresses this as he has one move to the location of the list of gifts that were identified by the assessment (p. 99). Then, the results are charted to refine the list to the most significant areas. The gifts and the tasks that relate to them are matched so that the person has a direction that can lead them to effective, fulfilling ministry.

As stated earlier, there are many assessments, and each one has great value in its own way. We have just lifted up one that leads to specific areas that fit our contention with regard to service. Schwarz specifically cites *service* as a gift of its own. We are declaring that all gifts, in some way, should be of service to the Kingdom of God. What we want to convey is some methodology to make this happen for you. A healthy church will have a balance of gifts, of some sort; but it will have some that are more dominant, both effectively and ineffectively.\

So, it is possible to use the charting of each person surveyed and chart the group to come up with one for the church. It is also possible to do this in a simpler way that will give you enough of an idea of which direction you should head. The problem with DIY in such situations is that there is a good bit of subjectivity that comes into play when you don't allow an outside source to tabulate the results. It doesn't seem that there is a great danger in using your own methods to get started. You can still obtain results that guide the process in the way it should go.

Focusing on Your Own Gifts

In the end, you will have to decide how you plan to approach the task ahead. It may be that your church decides which path to take on its own. They may just not do anything in the way of a church-directed objective. Nathan found himself seeking a project that he felt passionate about that didn't fit with the church where he was a member. This wasn't a rebellious move; he was entrepreneur enough to plan the strategy, assemble a group of like-minded folks, and charge forward to take on the challenge. A lot of the rest of this book is about doing just that. It's not for the faint-hearted or those who need a lot of outside support to take this on. That's not necessarily bad, but be aware of the tendency to settle back into a complacency mode. God offers us opportunities all the time, and we need to discern His will in such matters.

Olympic skier turned quadriplegic, Joni Eareckson Tada said: "My enforced stillness has led me into a deeper firsthand knowledge of God through prayer." Along with all the books that she has authored, she managed to create a ministry that sends repaired wheelchairs all over the world to give to those who cannot afford to purchase them without her help.

One of the ways that we can miss out on blessings that God offers is to decide that something is just "not your thing". We wrote about that earlier. Here's an example of this that happened to Nathan:

> He had been in the Walk to Emmaus movement for fifteen or so years. He moved on up to the highest levels in the community he is in. A person who was serving in the Kairos ministry asked him to be a member of a team that he was leading. Nathan had often said that he was just not cut out to be a part of a ministry that is held in a prison. He had never had any dust-ups with the legal system and didn't feel that he had anything to offer. If it had been anyone other than the person that called him, he would have probably found it easy to say "no". After becoming a part of that team, he is now feeling that he has been blessed in ways that can come from no other experience.

Since Nathan's experience, several others in the community have participated in a Kairos event. Certainly, it is not for everyone, but there are ways to serve that don't involve being locked in for four days (not overnight). A vicarious involvement can be very meaningful in its own way. In Walk to Emmaus, he has seen many people who didn't want to share their stories or to get deeply involved in other ways find that the Spirit can lead them in ways that can draw them closer to God. In many cases, people have found that gifts that they didn't know they had come in full bloom. Understanding that you are gifted in a way that brings glory to God can help you find the purpose that He has for your life.

Here's how Schwarz breaks down gifts into three areas. This follows the overall scheme of his approach: a Trinitarian way of showing the nature of your relationship to the divine. He uses colors for each of these natures, and we will show you how the gifts fit into each one. Here is how they are broken down:

Wisdom – green	Commitment – red	Power – blue
Artistic creativity	Apostle	Deliverance
Craftsmanship	Counseling	Discernment
Giving	Evangelism	Faith
Hospitality	Helps	Healing
Knowledge	Leadership	Interpretation
Mercy	Missionary	Miracles
Music	Service	Prayer
Organization	Shepherding	Prophesy
Voluntary Poverty	Singleness	Suffering
Wisdom	Teaching	Tongues

Certainly, there is more to this process than taking a test and then plugging yourself into where your gift falls. One needs to open one's heart to God, to be ready to apply one's gifts, to get informed, to begin with, what one enjoys, to experiment as much as possible, to verify your effectiveness, and to seek the opinion of others. If NCD is the approach you choose to take, the book, *The 3 Colors of Your Ministry* is the guidebook to conducting a full-blown assessment. If you seek the counsel of someone who is well-versed in doing spiritual gifts assessments, they can give you a very solid process to follow.

Taking Action

Once you have completed the assessment and determined the route that you should take, you are ready to move on to the next step: how we decide where to begin to use our gifts. There are various ways that this can be done, but the most effective way seems to be by gathering with other like-minded folks. As mentioned earlier, service is a spiritual gift, but it involves other gifts as well. Therefore, every group benefits from Christians who exercise this gift. (p. 120) The nature of this gift is that it enables Christians to recognize where their participation is needed and to make sure that the most urgent jobs get done. These people may not want to be leaders; they may just want to be directed into something meaningful for them.

So, this is the main focus of our thinking on this matter of *service*. People with a particular gift don't always know how that fits in with the larger picture. Let us give you an example of a multi-faceted operation. It also happens that this is a project that Nathan helped to start in rural Missouri. The original concept was to locate a setting for a retreat center where training could be conducted in a serene setting. This center would be for the purpose of helping those who want to be entrepreneurs receive training while exploring different ways of approaching their area of interest. The difference in this project was to be that Christian values would be infused into the training. The prime focus would be on customer service, with the feeling that this would give the trainees the ability to be hospitable (Spiritual gift) while helping to counsel (another gift) customers in matters of faith in a relaxed setting. This notion came from a coffee-house format that has been used in many different applications in many different locations.

It wasn't long before it became apparent that the best way to do this was to have a working model to use in the training. At an event with Pastor Bob Bullock, Nathan broached the subject of locating this project in an area with the setting for training where business development could use a shot in the arm, so to speak. Bob immediately mentioned the church where he was serving at the time. After some research, Nathan found a great spot for the retreat and joined the church where Bob was pastor. Efforts to interest the church members in the concept went nowhere fast. Since the area around the hamlet where the church was located was in a similar state, Nathan found a way to get involved with some groups that were trying to improve the economic situation in the area. In order to get the *horse* (the working model) established first, Nathan proposed a plan to some groups and then to the main economic development organization. This organization had the responsibility of directing funds from the electric utility after the cleanup of a dam breach.

This part of the story will be abbreviated at this point, but we will pick up on it later. The point here is to describe the plan as it relates to groups that were to be involved in the operation of the facility proposed. Originally, the concept was to center around a coffee shop patterned after one in the St. Louis area. It was started by a physically challenged man who has a heart for helping others with similar disabilities and those with mental disabilities as well. He was raising funds to help those in need while providing training to the workers he had at no cost to them or their families. His operation had been a shining star in restoring dignity to those who had lost it through no fault of their own. It still is, and he was ultimately very helpful to Nathan in getting his project underway. However, local politics got in the way and changed the direction of the project. The creativity that was utilized in making the direction change has made the operation self-sustaining while helping people in various ways.

This is where the gifting aspect plays a part. The project changed from being a coffee shop to becoming a café as a gathering place with a training facility component. The funding was allowed to be used for such an activity, and there was some concern about the reaction of local food service businesses. You see, this has become a *social entrepreneurship* project. In order to qualify for the amount of funding required, all of a sudden, Nathan's desire to train entrepreneurs kicked into gear. Again, for purposes of making this cogent to the point at hand, the project had taken on a small business incubator, a coworking area, a number of spaces for meetings and events, residential housing, and a future business and visitor center, including private mailbox services. Now, the requirement for various backgrounds and gifts comes into play. The main reason is that the witnessing and counseling aspects are quickly bubbling up to the top of the organization. However, this enabled the board to draw in several different groups to make this operation effective.

Certainly, there are a myriad of ways to approach such a major endeavor. With Nathan's varied background in business counseling and teaching combined with a long history of entrepreneurship, this project has reached many of its initial goals. It has been a project with many twists and turns; but God has been in this, making the effort effective, and has blessed those involved. More about that will come as we move into relating the full spectrum of such projects. The learning process has been amazing and exhilarating as well.

No one really expected the project to move in the direction it did. There were those who didn't want the project to succeed. The reasons are varied for this push-back, but it mostly has to do with four types of people who may be: lethargic, apathetic, lackadaisical, and\or anti-capitalistic. You can find a more complete explanation in Appendix B.

When you are interviewing a person that might be a fit for a team to create and implement a project, it would be good to find out what their goals are before you try to put them on the team. The purpose of a consultant is to find out what is going on in a business so you can help them find ways to achieve their goals. It's important to remember this when you go to consult with a potential client. Hopefully you are there to actually help the client and not just there to make money in the engagement. You see, there are times when the perceived goal is not what the client wants. Everyone has this *bag of tricks*, and you would do well to try to prepare for what comes out of the bag. Some people would be really put off by the experience that Nathan had when he first went to help with Habitat for Humanity. It was something that needed to be done, but it was a breakdown in communication or an example of just not caring. Had it not been for Nathan's determination to continue to work with the organization, he and others may have decided that it was a waste of time.

The apostle Paul told us to keep alert and persevere (Ephesians 6:18), and this is something we will revisit often as we move forward. Servanthood is a journey, not a destination. It's what we must be about all the time.

"Every Christian should understand the way he or she has been gifted and then put those gifts to use in ministry. Having been made for God's pleasure, we can then live to His glory."
Christoph Schalk

CHAPTER 4

How Do We Decide Where We Will Get Involved?

*"Each of you should use whatever gift you have received to serve others,
as faithful stewards of God's grace in its various forms."*
1 Peter 4:10

Discovering your spiritual gifts, as liberating as the experience is, provides only fodder for head games unless you find your way to unleash them to make a difference. Robert Lupton says that even at five years old, children have a notion that they are built for a purpose and that they have the power to make a difference. Unfortunately, at that tender young age, most don't find their way to the path that will take them where they are destined to go until something unlocks that power inside them.

For Nathan, it took over fifty years to get to the point where all of the experiences of his life came together to shine the light on his divinely- created passion. Naturally curious, he found himself early in life chasing after new products or ideas with reckless abandon. He examined things to determine how they worked and sometimes left these things irreparably changed. You can probably imagine his mother's consternation when a perfectly good toy was no longer useful. Oh, but Nathan would find a way to use the pieces to make something useful. Most of them weren't as attractive to the eye as the original, but the joy of the creation was much, much better. His parents mercifully presented him with an Erector set so that he could make his own creations without destroying something first.

It would seem that God as Creator knows the joy of what He has made. In Genesis 1:31, on the evening of the sixth day, we are told that God "saw everything that He had made, and indeed it was very good." Unlike the suggestions of some theologians, most believers accept the idea that God still creates. His hand may not be in every direct aspect of the action, but He oversees this ever-sustaining process through His creative power. We believe that God has put much of this into creation itself, thus giving much of Himself to His created beings. Not that we are gods ourselves, of course not. However, the spark of the divine in each of us is a revelation of God's self.

Think of a time when you made something yourself. It may not be a masterpiece, but it is unlike anything else ever created. Early in your life experience, it may not have mattered whether it was good or not – you made it. Nathan recalls his old-maid aunt, that took up painting very late in life. Realistically, her creations were not particularly noteworthy, and it doesn't seem that she stayed at it very long. Most of us are like that, and we feel pride regardless of the quality of the creation. We can, however, revel in the experience. Try to remember what you were thinking as you made whatever it was. Oh, it doesn't have to have been a thing; it could have been an activity you created or learned how to perform. However it happened, you probably invested a significant period of time and energy in the process. The point is that it was the journey more than the destination that gave you pleasure and, perhaps, pride.

If you have spent any of your life attempting to help someone else accomplish something, then you know that it can be both frustrating and satisfying. In some ways, we are our harshest critics, but in being so, we try to protect ourselves from the criticism of others. As we trudge through the trials and errors of creating something of value, we may just want to shuck it off. After all, life is short, and we may not waste time on a creation that falls short of expectations. Of course, then, there is Thomas Edison. He is said to have responded to a question about his lack of success in perfecting the (light bulb) by saying that he now knew 1,800 ways that it wouldn't work. As the story goes, the next attempt was successful. Most of us won't go through 1,800 tries to attempt to achieve our goal, and that is unfortunate. We never know what lies around the next bend. How will you live with that?

What About Research?

Who goes off on an experimental junket without at least doing some background checking on the task we are undertaking? A lot of us do, actually. Nathan was reminded just recently of the concept of "ready, fire, aim". That is appropriate in some instances, and it is better than procrastinating yourself into a false sense of inaction. Research can make the job much easier to accomplish, but it does require time. Only through careful consideration can you decide on your approach. If you have ever seen or known of a house built in a day? It has been done. There are corners that must be cut, but the point is that the planning that went into the process was the key to the ability to accomplish it. It takes research and experience to pull off such a feat.

Research doesn't have to be formal; it can be the accumulation of experiences that provide a bank of information. Some things become almost rote, and *throwing something together* doesn't have to be the manner in which the task is done. Just think about a task that you do on a regular basis. If you really want to see how this process works, try to write a script of every movement, statement, etc. that goes into a simple activity. Don't leave anything out! Now think about how that would work if you had to consider each of these items every time you did anything. Mind-boggling, isn't it?

Getting Focused

So, pointing yourself in the right direction to get about this service thing doesn't have to be a monumental challenge. Nathan found that his experience in carpentry work as a young boy helped in many activities that were necessary in other situations. He built what is known as a *head gate* for a 4-H Club project. This is a device that is used to hold a cow's head in place while something is being done to them that they don't particularly care to have done. He used the construction of one of these as the object of a demonstration that won him first place at the state contest. This skill also helped him as a buyer for a hardware distributor and the owner of a hardware/building materials store. Additionally, it was very helpful on mission trips to repair the houses of needy owners.

For many of us, being made aware of our gifts opens the door for us to focus on potential places to serve. Once again, there is not always a clear path ahead. One approach is to brainstorm with friends, associates, fellow church members, or any group that feels led to help others live a more fulfilling life. Finding a goal or objective to seek is a great way to start your thinking about serving. Consider a park that could use some dressing up in a declining part of town. This could be the impetus to launch a much larger project that could lead in a number of directions.

One of the biggest challenges is finding a good starting place. We talk about this in Appendix D. Of course, God will send up opportunities that give us direction. We must be paying attention in order to pick up on the clues. Nathan is one of those people who like a challenge, and he has found himself in some *interesting* situations sometimes. Being discerning will be a definite advantage when choosing the direction you will be taking. As you move through the process, you should learn many things that will refine your direction in amazing ways. Try to avoid overstepping boundaries that help protect you from getting bogged down. What we are referring to is the tendency to *rush in where fools tred*. Another problem can be the desire to control things to the exclusion of reason. Failing to plan means planning to fail, which is another pitfall.

When some group comes along with a suggestion as to how you might get started, it would be very good to ask a lot of questions. Ideally, the planners would put together some sort of matrix that would enable them to pinpoint the skills required to successfully accomplish the tasks involved. This seldom happens. In fact, many times, a live body is the primary requirement, with the availability of sufficient funds to pay their own way is a very close second. We have personally seen how disorganized a trip can be when sufficient planning and coordination are lacking.

An Approach to Consider

Let's look at some opportunities that might be of interest to you:

- Service in the church itself – Earlier, we spoke of the juxtaposition of *church work* vs. the *work of the church*. Perhaps the main consideration here is: Is this for just taking care of general tasks within the church, or is it actually helping other members become closer to Christ? Certainly, copying the bulletins or helping clean up after meals are necessary, but other than showing the stewardship aspect, there isn't much to be said for furthering the Kingdom. Preparing meals for shut-ins or for hospitality to visitors that's a bit different. Yet, and still, it is shepherding the flock. Not a bad thing, but too many churches seem to get inwardly focused by only focusing on these activities.

- While making a meal for someone can go a long way toward lifting their spirits, there's nothing like a *sympathetic* ear to give them a way to share their pain and/or anguish. In many cases, we find that offering a book on the subject that describes their needs can be extremely beneficial. Some can't or won't read, so perhaps a book on tape or just directing them toward a program on the radio or television featuring a pastor or ministry that has helped them would be good. Don't be afraid of questions that you can't answer. While 1 Peter 3:15 tells us to be prepared to share our own experiences, there will be times when answers are just not part of our repertoire, and we must draw on more authoritative sources. It's fine to refer them that way or to research the concern and report back to them. However, you must get back to them with what you have found.

- Reaching out to the unchurched – Your neighbor (literally) could benefit physically and spiritually if you visit them when they are sick or take them a meal when there is something going on in their lives that causes them to be under stress. Perhaps they have a potential divorce on the horizon or have found out that they have a terminal or debilitating illness. Just being willing to listen can be of tremendous benefit to them. Stephen Ministry volunteers offer confidential listening to those who really need to have spiritual healing to help them through the struggle that they are experiencing. If they need to have a pastor help them, try to connect them with your pastor or recommend someone (like a chaplain) that can help.

- Being more specific in connecting your gifts with opportunities – The three groupings noted in the previous chapter offer some guidance as to where your particular gifts can perhaps be directed. Many of us have gifts that lie in more than one of these groupings. Prayer and careful consideration can probably help you determine which direction to pursue. Where we are headed with this is to look at the needs within the particular ministry or situation that seems to draw you to it. For example, let's say that you are talented and gifted in the area of music. In St. Louis, there are some performing musical groups that take time to work in schools to help to develop young musicians. There's nothing like a personal approach to youth that needs some individual attention.

- Helping struggling readers has been a focus for many willing adults. Beyond reading, there are disciplines that students need as well. These are obviously mentoring opportunities that enable a close connection to young people who may have many distractions in their lives. The objective here is to draw closer to them in order to offer them a caring hand to lift them to a level of dignity that may have been missing in their lives. In his role as Director of Next Generation ministries, Jeff has found that youth struggle with many esteem issues.

- Support groups – Perhaps you prefer a group setting to dealing one-on-one with others. These can be a bit stressful if the group deals with issues that involve some intimate aspects. Be careful to match your gifts and /or inclinations with the situations you will be dealing with. If the group is established, you can spend some time chatting with the leader, who can help determine if you are suitable for their particular situation. Your pastor or other spiritual leader or counselor could also be a source of guidance in such matters.

- Support groups – Perhaps you prefer a group setting to dealing one-on-one with others. These can be a bit stressful if the group deals with issues that involve some intimate aspects. Be careful to match your gifts and /or inclinations with the situations you will be dealing with. If the group is established, you can spend some time chatting with the leader, who can help determine if you are suitable for their particular situation. Your pastor or other spiritual leader or counselor could also be a source of guidance in such matters.

Major Projects to Consider

So, all of the above are basically individual, one-on-one opportunities (except the last one). While some of them generally lack the potential for any great difficulty in managing, larger projects that are handled by a group or a team can be very challenging. They require a lot of planning, research, and recruiting. They probably require substantially more money than the ones previously cited.

Luke 16 ministries focus on the three main areas of a person's life – physical, creative, and spiritual. These are basically the same as NCD's gifting areas. We feel that these areas need to be in a position of balance for a person to function in a reasonably normal manner. Housing (physical) may be inadequate, the situation insofar as offering the fruits of a job or other occupational track is insufficient, and spiritual life is not focused on the only source that matters. The person may be so distracted that they aren't able to function effectively in their role as a parent, spouse, or caregiver. Sadly, there are many cases where this is the situation. It's really hard to do much for these people. The key is to *stop the bleeding*, so to speak, so you can begin some sort of restorative path. In reality, most people have to hit bottom before much can be done for them. Otherwise, they will stay in the rut they are already in. For those where the problem is just one of the three, assisting with the one may be just what is needed to help restore the balance necessary for a healthy lifestyle.

The Dignity of Profit was directed at mission trip events that normally involve either multiple members of a particular group or perhaps that plus some individuals that choose to join another group. In either case, it focuses on going somewhere to do something for somebody. This could be housing rehab, clearing an area for a park, etc. The point is: it's a group thing. I use the word group because it doesn't have to be particularly cohesive. In other words, these folks come together for a purpose, and it is most likely *one and done.*

One particular aspect of such events could be that there is some outside organization that coordinates this. The leaders of these groups reach out to churches and other benevolent groups in order to address some need that has been identified. They may be due to a catastrophic event like a tornado, hurricane, flood, etc. An example for us in Missouri was the tornado in Joplin in 2011. Church groups rallied members from all around Missouri and others nearby (and some far away) to converge on Joplin for an extended period of time to try to aid the recovery of a once well-established area. Nathan was there with a group called Operation Blessing, and Jeff was coordinating the members of the United Methodist Committee on Relief (UMCOR). The operation was pretty well coordinated, but working with volunteers who have various times to commit to the effort still offers some major challenges.

Robert Lupton wrote in Toxic Charity that too many times charitable souls decide to treat a chronic situation (poverty, homelessness, and the like) as a crisis (natural disasters and such). In doing so, we throw all sorts of resources at a problem that has likely been going on for decades. There doesn't appear, in most cases, to be a real desire to handle such cases appropriately. We know that this may come across as being somewhat uncaring, but nothing could be farther than the truth. Constantly treating people as if there is no way that they could ever care for themselves robs them of their **dignity.**

Joplin was like most of the smaller Midwestern cities: businesses come and go, sometimes a factory that had been a mainstay of the area cuts back its workforce or closes, or perhaps a large operation is sold to an out-of-town conglomerate. Downtown areas all over the country have been drying up for years. Children grow to be adults in a locale that is barely recognizable when they come back from college or the military. Property values decline as older people age out of their homes and move in with relatives or to a retirement-type facility. Lower property values attract people who really don't care about where they live except for obnoxious neighbors and high utility bills. If things become unbearable, they move on, to another neighborhood or to another declining municipality. The tornado cut an amazing swath through an area that was home to dilapidated residential buildings and some fairly new and valuable property. Recovery was a challenge.

In the area where Nathan was working, houses no longer looked like anyone had lived in them. Some of them were vacant and had been for a long time. When the houses went into disrepair, many of them were sold (where possible) or handled in tax sales. However, many of them were occupied prior to the tornado, and the owners couldn't afford to rebuild them as they had no insurance. Multi-level rental apartments were the logical solution, but handling such *complicated* negotiations was not something that city officials were experienced in. It's not a criticism; places like Joplin don't sit around thinking about disasters. They should, but there are just too many other things that are pressing them at the moment. Nathan's flight instructor used to refer to *crossing bridges before you get there* as *practice bleeding.* No one does that because the subconscious keeps you from it. Therefore, the budget goes flat when a disaster hits, and money that comes pouring from donations and recovery funds gets beat around like a palm leaf in a hurricane.

To be fair, there are some groups that handle the re-building phases of disaster recovery. Of course, you never really recover completely. When Nathan had a business in Bridgeton (St. Louis) Missouri, a Good Friday tornado came through the area. Most of the damage was done to roofs and trees, which might not seem like a major issue. However, for months after the tornado hit, you could ride around the area and see colored vinyl tarps dotting the landscape. These covered the damaged area of the house roofs because the red tape stifled the process of paying the insurance claims. It seems that insurance companies wanted to pay for the restoration of the original roofs, and the building inspectors wanted all the updated codes to be applied to the repairs. Talking about adding insult to injury! It doesn't make a lot of sense since the roof was probably deteriorating all the more as the parties involved in the recovery sat around in climate-controlled offices trying to figure out how they could do the best for their organizations.

It's a good thing that we humans are a resilient bunch, for the most part. It's also good that we have laws to protect us from those souls who just hit their limit of what they can endure. On the other hand, for those who seek to achieve the highest possible level of recovery, there are some who take compassion on them. Some, however, just hang in there somehow with whatever they have been left with. When the time comes to vacate the house for whatever reason, decisions have to be made as to what to do. Many of them go the way of some of the houses in Joplin: too expensive to repair and resell for the value of what was invested in the restoration. Oh well, there's the tax sale where someone buys it for the taxes owed. Of course, they have to tear the dilapidated structures down.

Longer-Term Projects

Not every restoration is due to a natural disaster. Many of them are due to a lack of funds and/or interest in keeping up the property. Some people have the mistaken notion that a building that is declining by the minute is somehow going to miraculously be transformed into something worth having. It's hard to understand the thinking that goes into such decisionmaking, but it is quite prevalent. A lot of the problem, it seems, is that people just basically think about themselves and don't really care that the value of everyone's property is affected by those who refuse to care for theirs.

A lot of the time, churches and other charitable organizations make arrangements with their regional or national administrative groups to take on trips to locations where there is major degradation of the economic and community structures. Heck, there are even catalogs that you can peruse to find that *perfect* opportunity. These may be by a single group from a city or church or it may be city or church groups from all over the place. Nathan was a member of a church that had been working in a location in West Virginia for over fifteen years when he became the coordinator of mission activities. Several of the groups had some connection to the pastor, who had moved from one church to another until he arrived in St. Louis. This became an annual pilgrimage to this depressed area to try to better the lives of the citizens there. For me, it was really depressing to see just how widespread the decline had become. Additionally, it was demoralizing to find out how deep the problem was.

One of the church members from the church in St. Louis told of the reaction he got from one of the children he was working with. They were working on a flower garden at the entrance of part of the city. One of the local children asked him why he was doing this work. When the boy was told that it was in hopes that the local citizens would want to continue this type of work when the visiting group left, the boy replied that the parents would never do that. At the time, Nathan didn't know just how deep this problem was.

There was a gymnasium building that had been abandoned by the school. The state Department of education offered the city a grant of $70,000 to be matched by in-kind labor from the locals. Sadly, the locals refused to do it. It was mainly cleaning up and painting! The city was, however, quite willing to let the outside workers do the work so that they could get the grant. Little did Nathan know that this was a foretaste of things to come in another location and another time.

There were many cases in that location where the residents just didn't appreciate what was being done for them. They would sit around while workers were there and do nothing to help. Then, if something was not to their liking, they would complain loudly when there was nothing that could have been done to make it better than it was. Part of the problem is that residents were not required to help, as is the case with Habitat for Humanity.

"Alone, we can do so little; together, we can do so much." **Helen Keller**

CHAPTER 5

Is There A Better Way To Do Mission Work?

"We each carried out our servant assignment. I planted the seed, Apollos watered the plants, but God made you grow. It is not the one who plants or the one who waters who is at the center of this process but God, who makes things grow. Planting and watering are menial servant jobs at minimum wages. What makes them worth doing is the God we are serving."
1 Cor. 3:6-6 (MSG)

The short answer is "yes," and there has to be. Billions of dollars are being spent to perpetuate poverty. It takes dedication, but it also takes some really deep planning and coordination. It also takes a sense of community on the part of the participants. This seems to be the only way that you can expect to have the expectation that success is possible. The purpose of the spiritual gifts assessment for this application is to ensure that you have a mix of the different gifts to give balance to the group. If you are forming a group that includes nonbelievers, you can use a personality–type grouping. At least these help to prepare for the challenges that will arise.

The Habitat for Humanity format is actually very good as far as it goes. It is basically a house-building or rehabbing program. One of the best parts about it is that it involves the homeowner in several ways. Nathan worked for several years with a program known as Mountain T.O.P. (for Tennessee Outreach Project). One of the best aspects of the program was that it used a very systematic approach to select the homeowners. It also did all sorts of work on houses – construction, repair, and remodeling.

Probably most importantly, it kept local construction people available to work with the crews that came from other locations to assist. However, local residents aren't working on the projects, for the most part. There is some rationale in this approach, but it underscores a major fallacy in such programs.

The *fallacy* is the way the folks that are the intended beneficiaries are selected. In many cases, it seems like there is a *solution seeking a problem to solve.* The West Virginia example features all of the things that are wrong with this approach. We mentioned the gymnasium rehab and the entryway floral garden, but even those are not the worst of it. The sense of entitlement that is created by this format makes it very frustrating to workers, and it alienates other residents who don't understand why they didn't get picked.

Mission teams aren't the only ones who find this so difficult to overcome. Local organizations that seek to help needy people create a better life for themselves, end up becoming jaundiced to the point of giving up or just going with the flow. In such situations, entrepreneurship is out of the question. In other words, why would you want to do anything for people who are not willing to do much to improve their lot? As a member of a ministerial alliance, much of the time in monthly meetings is spent deciding who is trying to game the system. Church folk typically want to help everyone who has a need, but the notion of socialism becomes less appealing when they have to give up something to give it to people who just don't make much of an effort to do anything themselves.

Once, Nathan had an experience in one of the no-frill grocery stores that was very frustrating. A woman had to leave a shopping cart full of groceries to locate more food stamps. This made a lot of people wait in line for her to return. The checker suspended the sale so that others could check out while the woman was away, but a lot had to be done to get the purchase back online when she finally got back. The total sale was over $500.00. Now, you may be different, but Nathan had all sorts of thoughts as an unwitting participant in this matter. Maybe she was totally legitimate and just not that organized, and perhaps that expensive jacket she was wearing was a gift or a purchase at a second-hand store. He didn't know, and he didn't like how the whole process made him feel. We are not to judge, of course, but how can you not question the display going on before your very eyes?

So, where this is leading is to try to back away from the fray enough to get a better view of the situation. A bin containing clothing to take to a ministry closet included a Lands End coat still in the packaging. Again, feelings that were probably inappropriate came flooding in when thoughts turned to how there must be a better way for this to work. It is a bit cumbersome to use other methods, but how about selling the coat at a discount to someone who uses the cash received to purchase three coats of good quality? You may be thinking that we are just swatting at gnats, but this is about restoring dignity to people who would be proud of something that was more appropriate to the world they lived in. If you are in a socialist country, having something of such value as the Lands End coat would mean that you are a target for theft.

There was a short story, The Gift of the Magi, by O. Henry, about a man and a woman who were married and didn't have much money to spend on Christmas gifts. The husband wanted a fob for his pocket watch, and the wife wanted a comb for her beautiful long hair. The wife didn't have much money of her own, and the husband lost his job before he could purchase anything. The wife decided to have her hair cut to be sold to buy the watch fob, and the husband pawned his watch to purchase the comb. In the end, neither could use the gift they received. They realized how foolish it was for them to want extravagant gifts in their situation. Perhaps we do a disservice to people who are very needy when we just give them something. Having something of high monetary value doesn't provide us with dignity – at least not for long.

Let's get back to the real point to be made here. It is extremely important to all parties involved that we choose our paths very wisely when we seek to restore dignity to those who have been robbed of it in some manner. These folks might be in a pattern of blaming others for their situation and believe that whatever they receive is deserved. Having a pity party is an exercise in futility since no one wants to go to someone else's party - they want to have their own party. Perpetuating a sense of entitlement or dependency does very little to encourage people to seek a more lasting outcome. Lupton suggests that helping people to **work** themselves out of poverty is **dignifying.**

The next section is about how to create programs or movements that will lift people up by empowering them to engage in becoming *profitable* themselves. What does it mean? In *The Dignity of Profit,* Nathan described how the Bible and even the culture of business define profit in other very meaningful synonyms. Some of these are: benefit, good, advantage, return, and gain. In some ways, this just doesn't seem to make sense; but in reality, it is extremely logical. Nathan also pointed out that we just don't do things for no reason – we normally expect some sort of positive result. Maybe some people just have to see the value in taking on a project. It makes sense to us because people should appreciate what you do for them. Gratitude is very important whether you are the recipient of a gift of some sort or if you want to show it by helping others.

Vision and Motivation

Motivation is crucial to getting anything accomplished – it is the *Why*. Without it, we are just merely functioning in some rote fashion, oblivious to any outcome that may be derived from the activity. We will discuss outcomes later, but at this point we need to have a vision of what we want to achieve. Jesus said in **John 11:49** (paraphrased): "You can see it if you believe it." Most people don't have a lot of vision. It is surely a function of experience and other means of becoming exposed to ideas and experiences. As Christians, we should try to take advantage of every opportunity that God puts before us. This is how we grow in our service and in our lives.

There is an example of how we can do this in our minds. Try to imagine the farthest distance that you can. Imagine what it is, and put a stake in the ground there. Then, imagine you are at that point and repeat the process. Entrepreneurs consider the idea of a flat rock being skimmed on a very calm body of water. It's a bit hard to keep up with things when they are happening so fast in that instance. However, if you can conceive how this is expanding your mind's reach, the outcomes will be much clearer when you seek to fill in the blank spots along the way. This is a bit obtuse, to be sure, but, again, this is a very powerful exercise. It is brainstorming at a very high form of consciousness.

A very effective means of fleshing this out is to make some notes while it is fresh in your mind. You won't get everything covered exactly, but the rest will come if it is a notion that has enough promise. It is important to let the desired outcome be the guide so you can vet this idea effectively. Nathan's experience has proven that your reach should always be shorter than your grasp so that you are forever exploring *new worlds* as you work your way through the maze of pitfalls on your journey.

An example of how this is necessary came to Nathan when he was in a church he was a member of. Nathan had been traveling in his work and just returned from an assignment where he had sensed a call from God that he perceived to urge him to go into full-time ministry. Once the assignment was over, Nathan knew he was not going to be working for that company any longer. He also knew that pulpit ministry was probably not what God had in mind. As he continued to explore the options, he participated in a celebration that was conducted with the church, marking a milestone in their process with Natural Church Development (NCD) - see earlier reference. The church had reached the status of being a *healthy church* by scoring 65% or higher on the latest assessment. It was a completely appropriate event as proposed by NCD, but Nathan raised a caution to the pastor regarding the tendency to become complacent. The pastor defended the process, and the next steps were undertaken.

The problem, as Nathan saw it, was that they were just making it over the line in terms of qualifying for the designation. His experience with retail store promotional events made him aware of the danger of peaking too soon. No more tests or training; the church had arrived. Not so fast. Greatness is not achieved by reaching some minimal level, and it was mainly compared to the other churches in the program. Additionally, the NCD program is based on levels of attainment based on eight quality characteristics, and there were some of these that really weren't that stellar. The pastor left the church and the pulpit ministry for several years. It wasn't really a bad thing; he had tried sabbaticals before in order to have a retreat experience.

Nathan had seen the value of the program because part of the celebration included a workshop where church members were asked to state what they thought needed to be done in light of their newfound status. So, Nathan met with the pastor to determine what the possibility would be to have him (Nathan) take over the program so that it would continue. Ultimately, Nathan was trained in NCD, but getting the church to do anything meaningful was difficult. When a replacement pastor arrived (after fifteen months with an interim pastor), the NCD program was shelved in favor of Appreciative Inquiry – at least it appeared so. The new pastor gave the book that described the program to Nathan to review, and he charged off on some other path, but it wasn't used either. Nathan still has the book; the pastor never asked for it back. It wasn't that it was inappropriate; starting a new program meant that all benchmarks and progress achieved with NCD were out the window.

This story might seem that we are negating our previous contention of always reaching beyond our current level, but that is certainly not the case. NCD does lead you in new ways, especially if you need to look at other characteristics for improvement as well. Specifically, the one that needed attention the most was *need-based* evangelism which coincidentally was the minimum factor in the first round of assessment! Also, this seemed to Nathan to be a very effective way to address the outreach needs of the church, and it was what interested him the most in his first review of the program.

There is a saying that goes like this: "If you always do what you've always done, you will always get what you always got." We feel like both of us are called to be *change agents*. Another saying is: "The more things change, the more they stay the same." So, how can that be? Well, it can because the old methodology doesn't work with new issues. It might put a Band-Aid on the problem, but it comes back stronger than ever. An example of this would be a workaround with a new product or method of doing something. Forty years ago, walk-behind power lawn mowers had a dangerous shortcoming: the feet of the operator could slip under the deck of the mower. In many cases, toes could be cut off when the foot got underneath the edge of the deck. However, when a guard was placed on the back of the deck to prevent this, people would take the guard off. Why? The guard had to be made so that it didn't allow feet to get close enough to the edge of the deck. Lost yet? The bottom line is: people would take the guard off because they were stepping on it. There didn't seem to be statistics published on how many people got toes cut off after the guards were removed, but Nathan had one. Of course, there was another contributing factor: the handles would fold down for storage, and the operator didn't tighten them enough when he used them. When the mower hit thick grass, the operator pitched forward, and he apparently stuck out his foot to catch himself. Handle collapses, foot goes under deck, and toes are cut off. Nathan was surprised that he wasn't sued over that, but perhaps the doctor recognized stupidity when he saw it.

Real Solutions

The big point here is that too many times, those who are seeking to solve a problem or improve a product or process, stop short of a satisfactory solution for the long haul. Obviously, there is a lot that we don't know about such matters, and that may be because of *grand design*. God doesn't care for us to know everything because humans would want to take credit for what God has clearly done. The "great" architects that built the tower of Babel found out that trying to take over God's handling of matters put them in a bit of a pickle. However, seeking and finding tend to go hand-in-hand when God has put us on a path to do something. The notion of putting a stake in the ground doesn't ignore the need for us to be doing something while we are waiting for God's timing. However, planting stakes doesn't put us in charge; it merely gives us a role in determining a path to the future. Otherwise, we are doomed to repeat the past over and over, expecting something different (the definition of insanity).

In his great book, *In the Grip of Grace*, Max Lucado tells the story of some brothers who decided to take off on their own against the wishes and advice of their father and the older brother. In order to get themselves out of the mess they were in, these brothers made choices that, except for one brother, led to their destruction. This was due to their decision to *do it their way*. All were very short-sighted, and they tried to minimize the extent of their situation. Lucado suggests that the problem for the losers was that they didn't really understand the concept of *grace*. The father and the brother (representing God and

Jesus) made a superhuman (of course) effort to draw them into the solution that was always available to them. Alas, the outcome was not a good one; but it was the one they chose. Their knowledge base was inadequate, but their determination to be in charge was the killer. He also reminded readers that we are human <u>beings</u>, not human <u>doings</u>.

Who Is in Charge?

How many times have you seen situations where events have been around for many years, and only the scenery changes? The Abilene Paradox, introduced by Dr. Jerry Harvey, provides some insight into how the inability to manage agreement wastes time and energy. In his anecdotal story, he shows how the default of leadership causes a decision that no one likes. One of the applications that seems all too familiar to churches and other organizations would be the choice of committee heads and such. In many cases, getting someone who will be in charge of a committee is a particular challenge on a good day. Once you get someone to take the job, you may end up enduring them for many terms – unless your by-laws mercifully term-limit them out. However, you then are back to trying to find someone to take the job. We have seen this over and over again. The incumbent may not be the best choice, but the rest are willing to put up with the pain and aggravation of another term because they don't want to be the punching bag themselves. It's sort of a vicious cycle, and there is no end in sight short of the death of the incumbent. When someone does follow leaders that need to have left long ago, the deck is stacked against them.

The sad reality is: most leadership jobs don't come with an instruction manual. If the previous leader was a strong one, members may be happy to get rid of them, and nothing will be done. If the previous one was a weak one, the committee may actually have been functioning on its own with no attention paid to the now-absent titular head.

Leadership for the Task at Hand

Schwarz suggests that *character development* should precede *leadership development*. It's vitally important that leaders be able to exercise good moral judgment. This makes leadership development valid.

Understanding the importance of ethical decision-making should be a prerequisite for leaders. Without a compass, it's hard to know the way to almost anywhere.

We found that leadership principles are not inherited or acquired by osmosis. They must be taught (or learned) in order to be useful. Team building exercises can be beneficial as well. Helping groups to achieve something together can be a real morale booster. Some like mixed teams when they go on projects, but others like the groups to stay together. When Nathan was in Boy Scouts, most troops stayed in cabins together at summer camp. However, they went to classes with other troops in some cases. Once, he had to stay with another group because he was the only one in his home troop at camp. It was OK, but he was treated like an outsider. The camaraderie just wasn't there.

When the tornado hit Joplin in 2011, there was tremendous support from church groups and organizations that routinely respond to disasters. There seemed to be a great deal of coordination in that event. Since the Joplin experience, both of us have had experience with similar events.

We mentioned earlier about the crisis vs. chronic struggle. Once all of the initial support comes in, a vacuum seems to be created that keeps the kind of support needed by some areas from dealing with the situation long-term. In the case of Joplin, many of the people displaced by the tornado didn't return. They were living in houses that weren't rebuilt: and even if they were, the cost of moving twice, the increased cost of living in the new structure, and the probable lack of a job kept them from being able to return. There have been some changes in how local areas deal with this potential; many people see this as crossing a bridge that they haven't even seen. The Federal Emergency Management Agency is charged with overseeing and helping in cases that cover broad areas. However, states are setting up agencies even down to the county level, and this is sorely needed to make sure that plans are made and carried out in the event of natural disasters. Nothing ever seems to get back to *normal* – whatever that is.

We serve ourselves and those with whom we have a relationship when we maintain the bonds that tie us together. Certainly, we should have strong ties with our Creator.

More Small Group Dynamics

Over the years and in many different locations, Nathan has seen a lot of the challenges that militate against cohesiveness in a small group. Take a Sunday school class, for instance. In the past, a group got together to talk about what they wanted the format to be. A railroad job is utilized to place the leader at the head. Some join because of the leader; others don't join because of the leader. Some members don't care about the leader because they are going to try to monopolize the class anyway. The group may grow, usually because of people who move in from another location. However, the group tends to top out over time. Deaths, people moving away, and people who get their feelings hurt or prefer another approach cause the numbers to dwindle. There is a point at which the decline becomes great enough to sink the whole class. There are certainly other factors, but you get the point. The exceptions have been the senior men's and women's classes. They are destined for precipitous collapse at some point. In many cases, it is due to the departure of the leader who had a long tenure in that position.

Nathan was once in a class at a 1600-member church. Initially, the class was rather cohesive. Most of the members were either about the same age or at least shared most of the sameaged children. The class had parties and invited some people who were not in the class but were friends or potential recruits for the class. The class grew larger, and other classes were formed when some of the members were not sharing the same activities at school or whatever as the others. The new classes gained new members, and the original class grew so large that it had to meet in the gymnasium. Teachers were recruited out of the larger class as their children went into middle school or high school. It later seemed that classes dried up when several of the members moved away at the same time. The members that had become teachers might still be with the original classes unless both spouses were doing something outside of the class itself. The original class was so large that their seating arrangement was theater style as opposed to a circle where everyone was looking at each other. There didn't seem to be any cohesiveness left.

This is reminiscent of college lecture classes where a warm body in a seat would ensure that any person sitting in that seat would be enough to avoid an absence. It is so easy to get lost in such situations. In many communities, there are so many people essentially *off the grid*, that getting citizens on board a movement of sorts is almost impossible. Groups formed to accomplish a task that will impact people in a meaningful way need to develop a sense of community in the very beginning. This not only helps to get people on the same page, so to speak, it helps get folks plugged into the right positions. It is, however, easy to mistake a well-placed set of workers, etc., with a *well oiled machine*. After all, people aren't machines, and today's culture resists being told what to do. It does work fairly well if people like each other, and there is not a problem of heads butting to see who calls the shots.

Non-traditional Groups

Traditional ways of grouping people in a church setting is rather haphazard. In *How to Lead When You Don't Know Where You Are Going: Leading in a Liminal Season,* Susan Beaumont shares some stories about how churches deal with changes in leadership and opportunities to rethink the way that a lot of processes, etc., are conducted. Both of us have dealt with a lot of different churches, Jeff as a *consultant/ coordinator* and Nathan as a church member and committee chair. Much of what goes on is more about personalities and/or keeping a tradition. Another great book is *Changing the Game*, the New *Way to Sell* by Larry Wilson. The opening premise is: If you are going to walk a mile in someone else's moccasins, you need to take off yours first. Simple concept, but it is quite powerful. It is, of course, a way of saying that one needs to get a look at the situation through other person's eyes as they go about their activities. You do still need to look deeper into what is probably going on there.

Perhaps the best way to form a new group is to get people to sign up for the groups they feel they can contribute to. There will be those who actually just want to be in charge of something but may not be a real contributor. It may be OK since they may have skills that complement the other group members' abilities. NCD has a program for Community development that includes an assessment of the energies that drive how people can best be utilized in a group setting. The concept involves utilizing these energies for good as opposed to being directed toward one of the seven deadly sins. The chart that describes how this works is in Appendix E. It is a radical concept in that most churches shy away from dealing with the problem of sin anyway. This is so powerful in that it redirects the energy toward a positive outcome. We will not go into all the aspects of the program, but suffice it to say that this is a new approach that can be very beneficial in group development. It is the way NCD addresses the quality characteristic of *holistic small groups.* The test that is used to provide the assessment can be very revealing, but it doesn't have to be fleshed out to be effectively utilized. The main purpose here is to create a balance in the population of the group in order to make it most effective and cohesive.

So, here's the point: being in a community is the design that God has for us. In order to be able to do that, we must have a relationship with those who are a part of it. Admittedly, if we are looking at a community in the sense of geography, the relationship is a bit tenuous. The type of community we are seeking to form is connected in some important way. In the case of the Christian community, we should share a relationship with our Creator. With that in common, we can move into a sense of community with each other. The shared goals should enable us to move into a stronger relationship in order to move forward together.

The real payoff comes when we can have multiple holistic groups within the church or other like-minded organizations. When the individual groups have a ministry in common, the synergy generated by the ministry is amazing. We used to call it *being on the same page,* but whatever it is, it's the energy being generated together. This could be a housing project where the individual groups have one common goal that fits in with the overall objective. Contractors working on a subdivision know how effective this can be. We once shared a business in common – an electrical contracting company. The general contractor would move their crews through the rows of houses, preparing them for the electricians and others to come through. This avoided losing a lot of time waiting or moving to another job. Everyone was a winner in such situations. There are jobs/tasks that don't lend themselves to this methodology, but every process can be improved.

For some other information on dealing with groups, check out Appendix A – Tribalism - which provides insight into some of the innate challenges that are faced in trying to create relationships that will lead to building community.

Making a Difference Where You Are

Perhaps you have heard the saying, "Bloom where you are planted." The purpose that God has for us is very time- and situation-specific. As we pointed out earlier in this chapter, all of us are unique creations of the Almighty. He obviously knows what He intends for us. The Parable of the Talents **(Matthew 25:14-30)** offers a look into just how God works with us. You are probably familiar with this parable, at least to some extent. The point to be made here is: each of the *servants* was given something (in this case, money) according to their respective ability. They were expected to make the most of what they were given. Two of them succeeded, and the third did not. Here are some points that Liz Kanoy makes about this point. We should:

- Recognize that God has given you exactly what you can handle for his glory in the place he has put you.

- Use what God has given you to the best of your ability for his glory.

- Avoid comparing what God has given you with what he has given someone else.

All of this is essentially about being faithful with the gifts God has given us, persevering, and bearing fruit. If your call is to go elsewhere in order to live out your calling, that is certainly appropriate. That is, if you are following God's leading. Remember, life is a journey, not a destination. We will be held accountable for each leg of the journey. God gives us detours sometimes so that the time and situation are right for us to produce fruit and give the glory to Him. More about this in the next chapter.

Perhaps you are hesitant to get involved in being a mentor. Brenda Rodgers makes an important point by writing: "Whatever your fear about mentoring – whether it's that you think your past is too bad or your story is too uneventful or you're afraid you won't have the words to say – remember that God qualifies the called. He doesn't call the qualified." Check it out. The Bible is full of *unqualified* people who *became more than they could be* by answering God's call.

"The very presence of vested neighbors committed to ridding their streets of drugs, improving educational opportunities, and restoring homes ignite hope and kindles visions of what the community could become." **Robert Lupton.**

CHAPTER 6

Is The Outcome Really That Important?

"He cuts off every branch in me that bears no fruit, while every branch that does bear fruit, he prunes so that it will be even more fruitful." **John 15:2**

One of the Six Growth Forces, as defined by Natural Church Development, is *Fruitfulness*. Schwarz notes that "this principle is about defining what *fruit* means before you even start a ministry, and a measure or program that does not bear fruit must be changed or dropped, and everything that does bear fruit must be improved so there will be even more fruit in the future."

So, to us, the real question might be: why would you want to do something that didn't have a good outcome? *Profit* was based on the premise that people normally don't do things for no return. There is a chapter entitled *Real Profit*, which is the original title of the book. The reason for that was to acquaint people with the reality of our choices of activities. Synonyms for *profit* were seemingly endless and helped to illustrate how our aversion to making a profit was misplaced. Some of the more obvious ones were mentioned in Chapter 4. These are all positive *outcomes* and make a lot of sense when considered as worthwhile endeavors.

You can probably think of some things that you might be willing to do for several of these, although it is worth noting that you just may be trying to be too altruistic. It is hard to argue that *benefit* is probably going to be a motivation in almost everything you do. When you were a child, you would have to admit that it would have been to your benefit to do what your mother or father told you to do – even if it were something you didn't like or want to do. The point is: everything you do has consequences, good or bad. OK, there are some that seem to have no benefit and are perhaps neutral. Nonetheless, you did them for some reason, didn't you?

We are probably all familiar with the statement: Doing something over and over again while expecting different results is the definition of insanity. In *Profit*, Nathan added that doing things over and over again and not <u>caring</u> about the results is immoral and may be criminal. Jeff's response to this suggestion came from reflecting on Missouri law. In his earlier days as a sheriff's deputy, an example was provided to help him understand the matter. What if someone gave you a cannon that actually would fire? You chose to fire it over a hill where you didn't know what lay on the other side. You did this every day until the police came to your house to let you know that your cannon fire killed an old man that lived on the other side. You would likely be charged with negligent homicide, don't you think? Now, we are not saying that taking away a person's dignity and creating a sense of dependency rises to that level. However, our insensitivity could be the cause of people losing hope when they are treated as if they have no place in our society. We are called to bring hope to the hopeless. What happens when we fail at our duty?

Dr. Sandro Galea is seeking to change the conversation on health – specifically, public health. When he was dean of epidemiology at Columbia University, he told the New York Times that the number of deaths attributable to low education exceeded the number of heart attacks in the year 2000. From our perspective, many of the areas that were included in that category were somewhat questionable. Primarily, it included those who hadn't completed high school. Other contributing factors that researchers found included poverty in a couple of different areas. Certainly, education and the effect that poverty has on the lack of it, are very important to health. In the aggregate, one of the key factors is the *lack of hope*. While it is very important that we address the causes of death, many times, the ways in which we approach finding solutions lead us to throw money at the problem.

The point here is that we probably don't give a lot of thought to the matter of poverty. In many of our cases, we have trouble getting our minds around this issue. There are a lot of people gaming the system, so we just see the poor as victims of their own actions. For those that find themselves in poverty, many of them just don't see a way out or they are so influenced by their surroundings that what they are doing makes sense to them. We say more about this in Chapter 8.

Jesus said that we <u>are</u> to love our neighbor as ourselves. If you are paying attention, you will see people in stores, on sidewalks, and in cars that only want to get to where they are going as quickly as they can without regard to what others are doing. In our way of thinking, not being thoughtful of others says volumes about the person who is guilty of that.

<u>Why Worry About This?</u>

Father Theodore Hesburgh, former Notre Dame University president, put the answer this way, "The very essence of leadership is that you have to have a vision." Perhaps the lack of vision is the reason we have a dearth of leadership in most organizations. Decisiveness is the hallmark of a strong leader, and many (if not most) people have trouble with that. Procrastination has a home in many of us. Surprise! Putting things off doesn't make them any easier. Being able to decide, however, requires the individual to have a vision that they can hold onto. Ever wonder where you get wisdom? The answer is: it comes from good judgment. The answer to where you get good judgment is: from bad judgment. That may seem like circular reasoning, but it is quite true. We seldom learn from success, but we can learn a lot from failure.

This book prepares folks to help others by creating a scenario that helps them do it for themselves. In doing so, it should restore lost *dignity*, and this should encourage them to help others. We are not doing this for ourselves – at least, we hope not. We wouldn't say that you can't be effective if you haven't had a lot of failures. On the other hand, it's quite difficult to try to help someone who is in poverty or has an infirmity if you haven't been there yourself. It is very important to understand what your gifts are and how to best use them to God's glory. To be really effective, you must also *learn to discern*.

Rick Warren said, "Unexamined charity – charity that fails to ask the hard questions about outcomes – only perpetuates poverty despite its best intentions. Responsible charity, on the other hand, engages not only the heart but the mind as well." We feel that the loss of dignity says so many things to the person to whom it has happened. It is a degradation of your value to others and to yourself. There can be a cascading effect on your self-worth that causes you to decline deeper and deeper to where the things that you do don't matter to you if only you can get what you want.

From the other perspective, our misguided motivation for giving may contribute to the problem. Andrew Murray puts it this way: "Under a sense of duty or from an inborn love of work, a Christian may be very diligent in doing his work for God, and yet find little blessing in it. He may think of gratitude as the great motive of the Christian life, and not understand that though it may rouse the will, it cannot give the power to work successfully."

Jesus poses the question in Luke 14:28-30 regarding counting the cost of a project before you engage in it. He asks if a person would start out to build a tower without first considering the cost. He is pointing out what the <u>negative outcome</u> would be if the builder didn't have enough money to complete it – his friends would laugh at him/her. This further adds to the decline in your value – your dignity.

It's hard to overemphasize the importance that we have placed on restoring dignity. In the location where Luke 16 Corp located the café and incubator, regularly during the day, people walk by going to the convenience store where they can purchase food, beverages, alcohol, and cigarettes. Some come by and have carts or other devices for transporting things. They could be going to the dollar store and expect to have more than they can comfortably carry. However, some of them are picking up cans to turn them in for cash. It's hard to know exactly what is going on in their lives, but many of them get enough from whatever assistance program they have. By purchasing alcohol and cigarettes, they are doing something that is injurious to their health and welfare. It was mentioned earlier that some of these folks use their money to entertain their "friends" to their own detriment. These people want things and to go places for pleasure, but there aren't that many opportunities. Therefore, they do what they can.

This area has opened our eyes to what hardcore poverty is like. Nathan approached the Ministerial Alliance when preparing the proposal for the Luke 16 project. Each meeting starts with a report of how many people have been helped and in what manner. While there is a great deal of emphasis on outcomes, the discussion has more to do with how to avoid enabling the folks that come for assistance. There are a number of benevolent organizations that attend these meetings, and each has a heart for helping people in need. However, a lack of willingness of these folks to help themselves stands boldly in the way of attempts by others to help them.

The café run by Luke 16 Corp blatantly projects its Christian values. Some people are turned off by that, but there is no preaching to any of the folks that were mentioned above. We welcome them, but few of them come in. There have been attempts to have worship services in one of the areas that is more suitable, but it is hard to get the churches to reach out to the folks we're describing.

How Is an Outcome Determined?

Yogi Berra is famous for his *Yogi-isms*. One of the more wellknown is: "If you don't know where you are going, how do you know when you get there?" King Solomon wrote in Proverbs 29:18, "If people can't see what God is doing, they stumble all over themselves, but when they attend to what He reveals, they are most blessed." The most any charitable entity can do is to make themselves available to assist in meaningful ways. Some of them don't really prescribe particular outcomes, but some do. Luke 16 Corp is offering training in customer service and also offering training/support to those who have an interest in owning their own business. Not all the people that have an interest in the training opportunities are like the folks described above. The idea is to be encouraging and provide assistance to help restore dignity and help people become contributors to society and not just recipients of the assistance provided by others.

There are a lot of factors that will affect the outcome, but having a vision goes a very long way toward being successful. Here are the things that can help ensure success as described in *Profit:*

(S)tandards

(U)nwavering determination

(C)haracter

(C)ooperation

(E)nthusiasm

(S)elf-sufficiency

(S)ustainability

These are pretty self-explanatory, so we won't spend a lot of time on them. Success is hard to define, but it is necessary to have an outcome to aim at. It's all a part of the *vision* since that is the real focus of our efforts.

Fruit-Bearing

It would seem that the whole notion of outcomes suggests that there is something being produced. If we set out to grow something, we expect that we will have *fruit* at the end of the process. The Scripture from the Book of John at the beginning of this chapter points out the importance of knowing what the outcome should look like. While that example was about apple trees, there are actually plants that are designed to keep the process moving. Murray points out that fruit only comes as "the life and the power in the Vine work in us. This alone is the secret of effective service." The capitalized *Vine* means that we honor what Jesus said: "I AM the Vine, you are the branches."

In furthering the notion of how important it is to understand the difference between work and fruit, Murray writes this: "We need to see that if work is to be acceptable and effective, it must come as fruit; it must be the spontaneous outgrowth of a healthy, vigorous life, the Spirit and power of Christ living and working in us." If we maintain our relationship with Christ as close and intimate, His nature will stream into us; and we will truly be *fruit of the Vine.* In other words, the fruit we bear is Christ's love.

A Holistic Approach

There is an organization headquartered in Springfield, Missouri, called *The Rainbow Network.* Their focus is exclusively on the people of Nicaragua, and they provide assistance in four areas: healthcare, education, economic development, and housing. Their structure is basically a co-operative so that each *member* pays back a portion of the cost of what they get. The approach is *holistic,* but it is only in one country. For an overseas operation, they isolate themselves from matters outside of the one country.

Admittedly, this is a very unique concept. It is also a vision of how *outcomes* can be attained and managed effectively. By dealing with virtually every major aspect of the lives of these people, they are looking out for each other. On its face, this may seem to be impossible in more contemporary situations; but we believe that there is great promise in the concept. In the U.S., however, the biggest obstacle may be trying to get people to work together for their common good.

Other Possible Outcomes

Charity Detox expressed some concerns about dealing with international situations. While they are, however, more common (and possible) in such locales, there are rural, and possibly certain urban, opportunities that could use some of the same approaches that were described.

This mainly had to do with *scaling,* the ability of a business to grow beyond its current state. This might be a small company that needs to move to the *next level,* or a larger company that might want to expand regionally or nationally. Much of the activity in these target areas is either geared toward the survival of the locals or toward lining the pockets of those who are only in it for themselves. This is not a recent phenomenon by any means. On the other hand, keeping people in perpetual poverty is not what we are called to do. Many well-intended projects do little to restore dignity to these people. Much of this could be accomplished by helping them learn how to do it for themselves and providing them with the necessary support. Scaling is not necessarily effective in those cases.

Lupton suggests that we replace short-term missions with economic missionaries. In many cases, these can be selfsustaining while generating income for those they serve. The attitude that many Christians have about money affects how they approach these challenges. Lupton counters these with a couple of powerful statements:

1. "We cannot serve people out of poverty."

2. "Making money with the poor is the highest form of charity."

"I would give all the wealth of the world, and all the deeds of all the heroes, for one true vision." **Henry David Thoreau**

In Chapter 9 and Appendix D, we will provide some specific guidance as to how to get involved in a meaningful way. All of these have defined outcomes to help volunteers pick one that is most appropriate to their local area and abilities.

CHAPTER 7

How Do We Deal With The Lack of Support in our Projects?

"Which is worse – ignorance or apathy?"

There was a story that made the rounds many years ago that involved a philosophy exam the professor gave with only the one question shown above. One student gave his answer right away and left the classroom. The professor generally didn't look at exam papers until all were turned in, but his curiosity got the best of him. He opened the paper to find that the student's answer was: "I don't know, and I don't care!"

We would like to add another item to the question: laziness. Most likely, you are familiar with the book, *The Little Red Hen* by Mary Mapes Dodge (Dodge, 1874). Perhaps you haven't thought about the Hen as being an entrepreneur. OK, it's a bit of a stretch, but she was trying to get others to join her in a venture involving a seed she found. It's a classic *reap* what you *sow* narrative, and it illustrates how human nature works. Why would anyone think that they deserved to receive any benefit (profit) from the Hen's work? But wait! That goes on all the time.

Jesus once asked if it was worse for a person to say they were going to do something and didn't do it or to say they wouldn't do it and then do it. Of course, it is better to follow through either way, but we don't really want people to tell us they will do something when they aren't going to. In the case of Luke 16 Corp, many said that they would work in the café. However, when it came time to do whatever it was, they were nowhere to be found.

Jesus also said to let your "yes be yes, and your no be no." It seems that being true to your word should be paramount. After all, Ananias and Sapphira lost their lives by not doing what they said they would do. God certainly proclaimed His opinion on the matter. This seems to be a tremendous lack of respect, not to mention a lack of commitment. Maybe that's where we are today; people don't want to be held accountable.

Volunteerism has taken it on the chin following a strong response when George H. W. Bush was President. He offered up a thousand points of light, which signifies the need to have volunteers as a part of our national landscape. There is a great need for people to step up to help fill the gap between the need and the supply of workers. In addition, community development depends on an adequate supply of people who care enough about others to give their time to assist those in need of support.

What a wonderful world it would be if people would give freely what they have in order to help lift others up. It seems that this is the world that God is leading us to. When we serve others, we are showing God's love. You may have heard it said that helping others is a cure for depression; however, people have to care enough to get involved.

The Ugly Truth

It seems to us that many people have a mistaken view of what it means to live out the *Great Commission*. Jesus called us to make disciples, not fix peoples' houses. OK, we know that working with people can be messy, but what else are we supposed to do? Earlier, we cited some examples of the lack of support from those we are seeking to serve. The instances are legion, and it's not really productive to try to presuppose all the scenarios that are lurking out in the mission field. What needs to be the focus is getting people on both sides to understand our mission.

Each group probably has a different mission. Certainly, there are many similarities, but in the end, people have something that drives them to serve others. It could be the very lofty goal of eradicating poverty;

such goals as that will most likely not be attained in our lifetimes. They could be simple goals like cleaning up a neighborhood. The problem with a lot of folks in our modern culture is that we want to get some recognition for our involvement. On the other hand, we may just want to do the task, savor the good feelings we have about it, and then move on back to our normal lifestyle.

You probably don't want to have people from either of these two extremes. On the other hand, you may need some of the one-and-done folks to fill in the gaps. If there is someone who wants to take over, you need to avoid them. They will fly in after things are headed in some direction and want to be in charge. This is not to say that other viewpoints are not necessary; clearly, they are. It is hard to be able to fly without a view from the *balcony*. The balcony folks, however, just don't have the true sense of what makes up the operation. It's like watching a movie and not knowing what is going on behind the scenes. The old saying that "you don't want to see how sausage and laws are made" applies in most situations. You know what we mean if you have ever taken a job or leadership role in a group where you didn't work your way up from the bottom. It's not that you can't function effectively; it's quite the contrary. It's that you don't know where the *bodies are buried*.

Nathan once said that he would never move to another location to take a job with a company he hadn't been working for. Of course, he did several times – slow learner, huh. Nonetheless, it is a tricky proposition. First, you have to get people to trust you and be satisfied with your character and your competence. When he took a job in St. Louis, he found that the company was almost completely different from what he had expected. It was partially due to the fact that the president interviewed him on a Saturday morning when only one other of the brothers who owned the company was present. They must have gone to acting school because the reality of their character and their relationship to each other were not very good at all, as it turned out.

Reasons People Don't Serve

Many people either don't understand the Great Commission (Matthew 28:19-20), or they just aren't interested (ignorance or apathy?) Charles Stanley spoke of how believers fail to serve God and weaken the testimony of the church. Here are some of the reasons/excuses for not serving:

- Ignorant of the Scripture

- Feel inadequate in their view

- Guilt-feeling

- Fear of failure

- Unwilling to make a commitment

- Lack of love and care for others

- Selfish with their time

- Comparing themselves with others

- Living in sin – no desire to serve God and others

We are servants of the grace of God, and it is our purpose to show that grace to others. As stated above, Jesus didn't put any boundaries on His Commandment.

Lack of Appreciation

While the points above are illegitimate excuses for not serving, there are some excuses that are not as much so. These are actual events that cause people to get very jaundiced about serving. These don't let people off the hook completely; they should be a cause for re-examining the process:

When Haiti had a real problem with cholera, Jeff worked very diligently to garner support for water filtration *barrels* that could easily be installed and maintained there. Many of these had to be picked up from the first recipients and redistributed to others. They were either not being used or had been repurposed for something that had nothing to do with the problem they were designed for.

- Nathan has worked with food pantries where the recipients either trade the food they get for money or drugs, or they leave things outside the pantry that they don't like. The shame of going to a pantry causes others to stay away, and some people go unserved due to some of the qualifying issues involved.

- Jeff received calls from a school in Haiti regarding a door that he had helped repair while he was there. The people he had worked with felt no responsibility for maintaining what had been made usable again, and they wanted him to do something about it.

- Numerous reports come from many locations about how people helped by mission trips in the U.S. do nothing to keep up property that has been either repaired or renovated.

This list could go on and on, but the point is always the same: people just don't seem to appreciate what has been done for them. Unfortunately, it goes way beyond mission trips. Most places have a sub-culture of people who are either flying under the radar or scamming the system somehow.

All of this makes it difficult to get volunteers who are willing to serve under these conditions. While it may seem that we are trying to discourage folks from volunteering, that is certainly not our objective. We need help in order to change the dynamics of the areas where service is so desperately needed. Stay tuned for some recommendations that will have the desired impact on these situations.

Keeping Your Vision in Front

You may be thinking vision doesn't really have any application to serving somewhere as a volunteer, but you would be wrong. Relationships matter. We touched on that earlier, but it bears repeating – over and over again. Nathan had a shocking experience when he first sought to volunteer with Habitat for Humanity. Shocking is probably not the correct word, but it was bothersome to say the least. He and his youngest son went to the headquarters only to find out that no one was expecting them. So, they walked around to some of the nearby houses to check for items that needed to be done to complete the project. No luck. By that time, it was lunch time, and the two of them walked over broken glass on the sidewalks to a fast-food place they didn't feel was safe to eat in. After eating, the two went back to the headquarters, where they spent the rest of the day making place cards for a dinner honoring the sponsors of the local organization. He's surprised that he went back after that experience, but dedication to a cause and a relationship with the church coordinator can drive you to keep trying.

The point here is: you must always be selling your vision. Even then, people move, some just drop out, and the hardcore believers are what are left. There was a story that was made into a movie entitled *Lorenzo's Oil*. It is a true-life story, one of those heart-wrenching ones that just naturally draw all sorts of emotions out of you. The gist of the story is that a young boy had a very rare disease that required a medicine that was only available in France. The company who had the patent made very little of it due to the low demand for the oil. After a lot of very difficult maneuvering and fund-raising, the oil was secured, saving the boy's life. The rest of the story is that the parents had become a part of the support group, which was led by the parents of a child that didn't live. However, unlike what you might expect, those parents weren't really interested in improving the situation beyond what had already happened. They were just keeping all the history of their child and their involvement in the support group at bay, so they still had a sense of importance. It is a bit sick, and it turns Lorenzo's parents off right away.

Numbers could be as high as $5 billion that is spent on mission trips of some sort each year. One of the most bizarre ones to our way of thinking was taken by a friend of Nathan's in St. Louis. The man was a widower and very lonely. He did some other things that reflected his desire to connect in some way to others. At his church, he did lots of work around the property and was present at virtually every event the church conducted. He and his late wife had been members of the church for most of their lives (maybe all). Nathan got to know him as a fellow choir member and then went together on a mission trip to Tennessee. It was a different kind of trip for him, one that was more like Habitat. People said that he might not like the format. He worked out fine, and he really enjoyed it because the food was very much to his liking. He even got to connect with some of the locals, which is what those trips are designed for.

The bizarre thing that he did was to go on a mission experience, of sorts, to China. Nathan didn't think he had ever been out of the U.S., and they stayed in peoples' homes when they left the major cities. We just couldn't imagine him doing that, and sadly, this really was more of a *working vacation* than anything else. He didn't say much about it, but he obviously didn't care much for the food or the accommodations. After that, Nathan began to see catalogs of such trips. They were all pretty slick with a great marketing pitch. A pastor that served a church where Nathan and his family belonged retired and became a *tour guide*. That just seemed a bit shameless. The idea is almost like a multi-level marketing operation where the guide's job is to get his friends to go on the trip and get his trip paid for. Without some point of reference, these *deals* might seem harmless. However, the money that is raised for these trips normally doesn't flow to the folks that should benefit from them.

Who's Doing What to Whom?

Up to this point, we haven't really talked much about the major problem with the service that people render to needy souls. Specifically, we need to consider the *dignity* aspect. In *Profit*, Nathan outlined how well-intended efforts to alleviate poverty fall far short of the mark. Some of those have been noted here. In the U.S. and other countries, people are actually rewarded for doing nothing. Jesus said we will always have the poor with us, and a lot of people must feel that they are helping do that. We can't imagine anyone seeking to keep people in poverty, but their actions are doing just that. Government gives away programs abound, and attempts to infuse some accountability in the mix haven't worked. In some areas, you would think that the days of the Great Depression were still around when you see how many people are finding ways to **not** work.

Previously, we have described the operation known as Luke 16 Corp. This is a 501(c)3, non-profit organization that was started to help provide training to young people who were interested in jobs in the hospitality industry and to help those who wanted to start their own business. In the area where this is located, most of the target audience is young people who don't want to work. They have to be paid to get their high school equivalency certificate. Many don't have a car to learn to drive on, so they just find places to live where you can walk to the stores they frequent. Many small towns around the area are just the same. If they can get to the grocery store, convenience store, and pharmacy, life is good. Many of the unemployed youth (and some adults) float around from one apartment to another where they can mooch off each other. If they can play their cards right, there will be one in the group who gets a check once a month. When they do, it's party time. A number of the recipients are suffering from some sort of mental deficiency or suffer the effects of alcohol or substance abuse. Rehabilitation and other well-intended programs generally just make the problem worse. Schools don't seem to really care about how many of them drop out as long as they can game the system. Many of them tout the achievement scores that aren't really that great, and most of the comparison is to schools that are similar to their own.

In many of the schools, the vocational education department is cranking out students that are trained for jobs that don't exist in the local area. This, of course, is not new. Nathan remembers how this worked in the early 1980s. In a recent visit back to that area, he found that a once vibrant city is now in serious decline. It's amazing that no one seems to care where they are going when they go through the motions in their job. Little by little, the economy dips into decline. If a family is not living in the area, many of the residents move to retirement areas, leaving their homes to decline in the hands of the lower-income residents who remain. The aspirations of those that remain are very low. It's like how a basketball will stop bouncing if there is no pressure on it.

The problem is exacerbated by the general decline that pervades most of the culture. There is no sense of the need to keep pressing forward. Lots of money is spent on entertainment, but even domed stadiums get torn down to do something different with them. Shopping malls, the once proud landmarks of economic activity and gathering spaces, have been in serious decline for many years. The difference between the northeast U.S. and the west coast stands in stark contrast to the rest of the country. Politics is trying to force people to live in certain areas to influence voting patterns. From the crowded neighborhoods of the major cities to the most desolate areas of much of the country, people just don't seem to have any sense of community anymore. So, what is it that we are about these days? Do we even care if we are really accomplishing anything significant anymore?

Is There a Better Way?

In the next chapter – Is Entrepreneurship the Salvation for Declining Communities – we will begin to provide some hope in such a dark situation. John Wesley once said that he couldn't talk about love and redemption without first talking about sin and rebellion. You would probably not like us to tell you how easy it is, but then you will find out that it certainly is not. It is doubtful that you would believe us anyway. The point in taking the side of the most difficult path is that you can prepare yourself and others for the resistance you will face. We think that avoiding being blindsided is a worthwhile goal. It is so frustrating to think you are making progress only to find out that the people you were dealing with hadn't put all of the cards in the deck. When it is to their advantage, they pull out these cards and trump your hand. God has to be in this, and He wants you to learn from experiences. The success will be His if you *play your hand right*. (You didn't think we were through with the metaphor, did you?)

If you haven't bailed by now, you will find some solid answers, but we still won't sugar-coat them. We want you to be in prayer about this and to lean on us whenever we can help. We want you to be successful too.

"The vision must be followed by the venture. It is not enough to stare up the steps – we must walk up the stairs." **Vince Havner, American Baptist preacher**

CHAPTER 8

Is Entrepreneurship The Salvation of
Declining Communities?

"...if we're concerned about moving the poverty needle, it will take more than community development and microenterprise. It will require for-profit, wealth-generating business creation." **Robert Lupton**

It seems quite amazing that so many people seem to dream of making a career out of being an entrepreneur. Both of us have had many businesses, and only one of these exists today, which was started by either of us. As of this writing, Jeff has a business that he started; and Nathan is serving as a consultant. You see, while Nathan still owns a business, it was not one he started – he just turned it around and made it profitable. Some of the businesses we have owned were startups, in fact most of them were. One of the main tenets of being an entrepreneur is *knowing when to hold them and knowing when to fold them.* An exit strategy is extremely important. You should always begin any project by starting with the end in mind. As an aside, Mark Cuban believes that an exit strategy is a sign of a lack of the obsession required to be successful. These two positions may not be contradictory; focusing on the future has to be part of a start-up plan.

In an article entitled *What Makes a Successful Entrepreneur: Perseverance,* Steve Tobak writes:

> More than anything, entrepreneurship is a game of attrition. It's about having the determination, the discipline, and the cash to

see it through. It's about not giving up and being the last man or woman standing when everyone else has fallen by the wayside.

While this is certainly true in most cases, success can be measured by various standards. In the case of *social entrepreneurs,* success does mean staying the course, and there is accountability. However, in such cases, it is important to consider what we are accountable for. For instance, small business incubators have been around for a lot of years in the U.S. These are facilities that offer free or subsidized rent to start-up businesses. They also offer some administrative services and some classes. Being able to fund and construct an incubator could be the initial phase for which the entrepreneurs are accountable. On the other hand, a paid-for building may not be worth very much until someone comes along and populates it with start-up businesses. It doesn't mean that the one who created the opportunity for small businesses was not successful in the task they were presented with. There should be some thought as to what happens next. Those who haven't been involved in an initial phase such as this one, don't know much about its success or failure. At best, they are just bystanders unless they were taking the risk of getting it built.

The reason for using this example is that it is all too prevalent with such incubators. St. Louis (MO) County built and operated as many as four of these facilities over a period of a couple of decades. Today, they are all offices for county government and other entities. Those who took the risk to get them built did their part. The managers who were responsible for getting tenants and helping them be successful deserve the blame for the failure. It was politics at its worst: corruption and ineptitude. It was not a failure of social entrepreneurship; that was never really their goal. This is really not that uncommon in many situations where the government seeks to try to solve a problem by throwing money at it. In the end, there was a lack of accountability due to the motive of no profit.

Since the Luke 16 project has been in operation, a new concept has come to our attention: the *accelerator.* It was interesting to note that this is a big part of what Luke 16 had in its planning. The concept is fairly close to that of an incubator; however, the one big difference is quite significant. Basically, the idea is that the *accelerator* is much more hands on. This starts to lean in to what social entrepreneur operation is like.

One may be thinking: how can they talk about social entrepreneurs and include a profit motive as a part of the process. It's actually because virtually every activity we engage in has *profit* as part of its goals. Many don't think of it that way, so the goals must be cloaked in something less offensive. Nathan cited Solyndra in *The Dignity of Profit*. This was the company that sucked in over $500 million to build a solar power operation that never made anything. As taxpayers and capitalists, we find this very objectionable. It fails on every important point. So, what was the desired outcome? I'm not sure there is an answer that makes sense short of graft. Who was asleep at the switch when the decision was made to engage in such a venture? How did they get away with it? All good questions. Unfortunately, there are no good answers that we know of.

Also in *Profit*, Nathan listed several synonyms for profit. As you consider them, you may ask: "Who could have a problem with that?" We could suppose that it is that they are just not viewing the matter that way. OK, so does that mean that just because you don't consider a tiger to be a man-eater makes it OK to be a house pet? Well, perhaps there are some, but that is not their nature. The nature of profit is not to be a bad thing. People make it that way by trying to *profit* from another person's troubles, or they just don't think that goods and services should be sold at a *profit*.

When Nathan was in a civic club many years ago, a speaker from the State Department of Economic Development came to make a presentation about the lack of knowledge on the part of high school students when it came to matters of economics. The results of their survey revealed the responses to two important questions. The first one asked how much profit a business should make on the sale of their product or service. The most common answer was $0. The other question asked how much profit most businesses make, and the common answer was 100%. We hope that you don't think that this is the case. If you do, you need to read *The Dignity of Profit* to find out the rationale for businesses making a profit. We have both been involved with nonprofits, and that is a misnomer. Being a non-profit means that the organization is not allowed to make a profit beyond its investments and expenditures. If they were only allowed to make an amount that covered those items just cited, every sale would be just trading money. Therefore, the organization would have to have donations for everything else – and even that is restricted.

We get what the reasoning is; there are many people who try to profit or gain from the operations for themselves. What would it be like if the goal was to get as much as you could so that you can do the most that you can with what you receive? John Wesley actually suggested that, and this is a man that gave away everything he made over his living expenses. It shouldn't be a goal to just trade money, but we have known business people who go into projects to just give things away. That scenario is a loser unless people have a valid need or will give it away themselves to someone who does. Otherwise, people can become dependent on the largess.

Here's one for you, courtesy of Dan Pallotta: an organization engaged Pallotta's fund-raising company to help them secure the capital they needed to expand their programming. The fund-raisers did a marvelous job, but the client didn't feel they should be paid the 25% fee they had earned. They didn't stiff the fund-raisers, but they fired them in favor of doing it themselves. Not surprisingly, the client cascaded down into the depths of financial despair. Back to the point of everyone losing, the client went out of business, the fund-raisers took a big hit in their revenue, and the intended recipients of the funds were not served. Who thought that was a good idea?

Social Entrepreneurs and the Problem of Poverty

In the U.S., start-up ventures have a difficult road to travel when it comes to getting the necessary funding and other support. There are programs such as the Small Business Administration (SBA) and some local programs targeted toward start-ups. Character and collateral are very important to lenders, and many young people haven't built up much in those categories. In rural areas where jobs are not available in a lot of areas other than schools or health care, there's just not much opportunity for these young people to put together what is needed to participate in the process. Unfortunately, schools go where the money is in terms of preparing the youth for a real job after high school. Nathan has lived and done business in several areas, and he has sold instructional computer systems to schools. There was a program in Indian River County Florida, that came up with what they referred to as a *performance based diploma*. Students who weren't mainlined spent the mornings in- class work to get them prepared for a high school equivalency exam. In the afternoon, they learned a trade such as carpentry, welding, or the like. It was a four-year program, just like traditional students, so they were completed at the same time as the traditional class graduated. While this was not in Nathan's territory, he was able to help some school districts in his territory to set up similar structures.

Today, these programs are much more common, but many of the trades being taught don't lead the students to jobs in the local area. Programs like *Work-Ready Communities* prepare students in such a way as to try to interest employers to locate production facilities, etc. in an area that would enable local students to remain there. Many students just can't wait for the area to provide the jobs for which they were trained, and they either commute to other areas or move to where the jobs are. Even some of those who commute find that they don't have much time to spend with their families and with local activities. Sadly, training is wasted on some who don't use it due to lack of local jobs.

Some communities try to re-engage with residents by having events that commemorate historic events or feature school bands, etc. Smaller towns and cities just have too much diversity on the one hand and not enough interest on the other to become a part of events. Volunteerism is at a bare minimum, and it is hard to compete with larger areas nearby. The lack of local merchants also minimizes the interest from visitors. A lot of this is due to what psychologists refer to as *learned helplessness*. The system at their level leaves much to be desired, and they don't feel that they have any power to change that. Many people that live in these rural areas just exist through government hand-outs or disability payments from somewhere. Most of these towns have virtually no way of attracting capital from outside the community.

Once upon a time, smaller towns and cities were able to garner support from locals when it came to offering fund-raising for diseases like polio or cancer. These charities have a more sophisticated methodology today. Once, when one of these organizations held a drive to raise funds, it was done by one neighbor passing the information to another neighbor.

Even in what has been a well-established area, many of these folks don't know one another. Even if they do, they may not like them. In the small town I grew up in down South, people rallied for causes. The racial changes in most of the South have altered the demographics and the relationships. It's not that they aren't better in some ways; schools and healthcare are certainly more available and of higher quality.

There are more factors than racial change. People are just more mobile. We are living longer, and that is stressing housing and other areas. We seem to be trying to remold systems to fit the dynamics of a new culture. Meanwhile, people are walking around with their heads in Smartphones and don't even care about what is going on around them. Recent reports have described what is happening to young brains that stay constantly connected via these devices. It's a dumbing-down effect, and socialization is confined to a small circle of "friends". It seems that a very large percentage of these young people just don't have enough drive to be able to even begin to function in the larger society. Smaller communities that feel they are OK, are on the verge of seeing a major decline in much of what has been going on there.

Many of these communities are looking for a factory or large employer to locate there. Sadly, there is a lot of competition for these, and the cost of admission to the event is generally too high. There is such a sense of dependency among the citizenry that most couldn't care less about economic development efforts. Drugs, multiple divorces, children that don't know their fathers (or even mothers) – all these combine to make life in many communities both dangerous and without the drive to become something better.

Community Development as Economic Development

The singer Bono has done a lot of work around the world. He has found that community development has to precede efforts toward economic development. This was mentioned earlier as part of the NCD program.

The International Economic Development Council had actually discovered that over twenty years ago. It has been reprised since Bono and others have rediscovered it. Many of these smaller communities will support community development because local banks tend to want to do that. The problem is that they don't seem to want to take the next step.

It is quite sad to see how school districts, which are the largest employers in most of the rural areas, can't see that the funding has to come from somewhere to cover the difference that they have to pay to educate the students. Some areas get some funding from government leases and other sources. Sales tax can do a lot to help bolster the funds they need, but there just isn't support for helping entrepreneurs to become merchants. Tourist-heavy areas like the one Nathan has been working with have disdain for tourists and don't generally support efforts to attract them. The last time we checked, Amazon, Wal-Mart, and other major retailers didn't do much for the outlying areas.

The commuting factor looms large when trying to encourage community development. These commuters don't have the time they need to spend with their families and to be a part of the community. Schools can be a cohesive factor; but without the parental involvement needed, assimilating into the community is difficult for most. Some folks start out by purchasing property for recreation, farming, hunting, fishing, etc. They may stay over weekends or for a week at a time; but unless they ultimately move to the area, there will come a time when they probably will have to sell rather than live there full time. They may never really become a part of the community unless they go to church in the area.

Timeshare properties don't help much. They get people to pay a large amount of money to essentially lease houses or cabins. It's hard to always be there on a certain week, and then there is the problem of weather not cooperating on occasion. Even before they tire of the same place/same time routine, many people lose interest in this. There is a cottage industry that attempts to help timeshare owners get out from underneath the burden of paying for the lease when they may not be able to take full advantage of it.

We know many families who have purchased or leased property to take the family on special weekends or just for a week or so in the summer. Nathan's in-laws had a cabin for many years, and some of the family still owns it. Since Nathan's family lived in Missouri and the property is in Mississippi, jogging down for the weekend wasn't usually in the cards. On holidays, someone would book it ahead of time, locking out the rest of the family. When some of the families got where they weren't going there very often, they didn't feel that they needed to pay for the upkeep of it. This led to some tension between those who did use it and the ones who didn't want to pay for them to do so. Partnerships of any stripe are difficult to maintain.

Jeff and his family have lived in the same area almost the entire time he and Nathan's daughter, Laura, have been married (except for a few months in the beginning). All their children were born there, Jeff has had several businesses there, and they have coached athletic teams their children were on. They have both been a part of a church family; they did change at one point to be nearer the home they had then (it was where Jeff grew up as well). All of their children went to the same high school and were very active there.

Nathan, on the other hand, was born in Mississippi and went to school there. When he went into the Air Force, he lived (with his wife) in Lubbock, TX, and Alamogordo, NM (where their first child was born). After that, he moved to Gaffney, SC, and then to Greenwood, MS (where the other two children were born). A move to the Jackson, MS area followed by a move to St. Louis, and then to southeastern Missouri. In almost every case, Nathan and Carolyn were very active in the church they joined, as well as being involved in the athletic and other events of our children and grandchildren. Some of the stays in these locations were short, and some were rather long. Both had a high sense of loyalty to whatever they were involved in. In many cases, one or the other of them was in a leadership position.

Building Community Is the Only Answer

"Everything in life revolves around relationships – everything. The most important relationship is a personal relationship with our heavenly Father through His son Jesus Christ – a vertical relationship…and the best horizontal relationships are covenant relationships to live with others, to become connected with others in a basic Christian community." **Rick Diefenderfer**

So, here's the point: connections to a community are not the same for people, whether they lived there all their lives, moved away and came back, or moved in from elsewhere for whatever reason. We have found that in the case of rural areas, there may be very few that are natives that care that much about the community. There could be a lot of reasons for that, but a few seem to bubble up regularly. These may be people who don't have a choice but to stay there. Perhaps they have a family that needs them, or they can't afford to move if they wanted to. They may have a job that is something that they don't want to leave due to the stability or salary.

The choice to stay may be for all the right reasons, but even then, they have a problem getting involved. A few years ago, Nathan formed Luke 16 Corp and got a grant to purchase a building to house it. When heavy rains came, and the building flooded, it was apparent that the previous owners hadn't dealt with the source of the problem. When he found out that they knew about it and didn't disclose that fact in the sales documents, he tried to get reimbursed for the cost of remediation. He was told that the old owners had friends that wouldn't like to have legal action taken. Wait! Is this the Mafia or something? No, it was good ole boy, down-home *redneckedness*. There is a lot of that going on around us, and not all of it is in rural areas. It is the way people deal with folks that they don't like, mostly outsiders, because locals know better than to cross those people.

If you think that the church is immune from such shenanigans, let us know, and we will provide you with first-hand examples and/or books written about how that can be. One of the greatest dream-squashers is the last seven words of the church – *we've never done it like that before*. A great book on this is one by Eddie Hammett entitled: *Reaching People Under 40 While Keeping People over 60*. One example was experienced by Nathan firsthand as well. It had to do with a church needing to create space for a nursery, and the only appropriate location was then occupied by the senior women's Sunday school class. Fortunately, both of the situations were resolved satisfactorily, but the journey to resolution was a rough one. It's something about communities, whether they are in or out of the church, that makes people feel like they *own* something that really doesn't belong to anyone in particular. That's how we get intransigence and why things don't get done.

After the 2011 tornado ripped through Joplin, MO, the city council was almost frozen in its inability to decide how to deal with the recovery. In the meantime, most of the people who were displaced left the area. In a way of transition to the larger picture, many businesses don't recover from such disasters. The multi-story hospital was rebuilt because it was moved five inches off the foundation. Insurance and donors made sure that it was done correctly. Additionally, the high school had to be rebuilt as well. It immediately struck us that businesses weren't going to fare as well. Some of that is merciful to hangers-on, but that's a hard pill to swallow for the owners who have put their lives in their business.

Iron and Reynolds counties in Missouri were given $7 million between them to rebuild property damaged or destroyed by the breach of a dam owned by the public utility. The two countries didn't work very well together due to the different viewpoints regarding how the money was spent. Reynolds County wanted to use it for public works projects, and Iron County wanted to use it to rebuild the portion of the economy that was affected by the breach. Four years after the money was awarded, the two split and formed separate organizations. The irony is that neither really did anything that affected the loss in tourism during the first six years of the recovery period. The tourism came back – due mainly to the state government spending their money on the attractions that were damaged. However, many of those who suffered the most just didn't make it back or had to sell out. As for Iron County, there has been so much wrangling over how to spend the money, they haven't spent even a third of the award. Nathan launched the project (Luke 16 Corp) to try to make an impact on the lack of jobs and entrepreneurial businesses that were needed to stabilize and grow the economy. Apathy, jealousy, and outright lies stagnated the growth of the operation. As new ideas have been brought forth to help mitigate the problem, more stagnation has been the result.

Challenges abound in trying to deal with these very thorny issues. We have spelled out a lot of negative examples, and it may look like we are trying to talk people out of creating entrepreneurial ventures. Absolutely not! We see entrepreneurs as the only real solution. It's just that there is a lot of work to be done in getting communities to understand it. After his first major experience as an entrepreneur, Nathan thought it would be great to be a consultant in order to share his trials and tribulations with prospective business owners. After a lot of introspection, he realized that the very thing that drives people to start businesses is what militates against inviting a consultant in. One major factor is the cost. Nathan's consulting fees have ranged from zero to close to $100 per hour. Even at that, you would think that paying a lot of money to a consultant would cause a business owner to pay attention to what they are being told. No, they are still determined individuals that don't believe anyone can save their business if they can't. It is usually a bank or spouse that makes the decision for them. It is rather sad that most consultants haven't been business owners themselves. Of course, that is why Nathan's fee was zero in some cases. It is also the reason (for the most part) that he chose to create a non-profit to help them. Just in case you think that that would be a slam-dunk, many don't even trust people who want to help them for free.

At its very best, entrepreneurship bubbles up from within a community, dedicated to making a difference in the life of the constituents. When people have their backs against the wall, they need to take a stand to save and revive their community if it is worth it. There are ways to do it, but people have to put aside petty differences and jealousy. An example of how it can be done on a large scale is what happened in Birmingham, Alabama. In his early working life, Nathan spent a lot of time traveling to and through Birmingham. This was in the mid-70s to the late 80s. For many years, the city had racial issues and was one of the nastiest places to live in because of the air pollution. The statue of Vulcan, the Roman god of fire and all things related to it, like metalworking, sat on Red Mountain, one of the highest points in Birmingham. The air was so filled with smoke and pollution from the steel mills in the city that Vulcan was barely visible. At its most productive point, the furnaces ran 24/7/365. When the operations that caused the problem lost most of the business, the burners were finally put out. They had burned continuously for as long as residents could remember. When they were no longer filling the air with smoke, the city was now faced with a new problem: how to replace the economic impact that the furnaces had created.

The details are not clear, but the air is. For someone who had spent a lot of time in the city when it was very unpleasant, the change was wonderful. IBM, AT&T, and others made the city a regional headquarters. There were two outstanding private high schools, two great colleges within a short driving distance, other economies near the city that were beginning to grow, a logistical crossroads, and an attitude that fueled the amazing transformation. Their solution in terms of details is not something that can be replicated, but the attitude can. A decision to not go down to defeat turned an undesirable city to a great one. Going back to previous comments: this is not a "one and done" proposition.

Now is probably the time to direct you to Appendix B and Appendix C. If you didn't read Appendix A earlier, read it now also. Jim Collins, author of Good to Great, said that you have to get the wrong people off the bus, get the right ones on, and then you can move down the road. It can make all the difference in the world, but you have to have the right people. Unfortunately, many times, that is not an easy task. The key is to persevere. No one ever accomplished anything great (or even hard) by giving up on it. If you can do it, you will be a hero. The world may not recognize it, but the One who matters will. That makes it all worthwhile.

"If you chase two rabbits, you will not catch either one." **Russian proverb**

CHAPTER 9

What's Next?

"There comes a point where we need to stop just pulling people out of the river. We need to go upstream and find out why they're falling in." - **Desmond Tutu.**

This _is_ about *service*, so you can expect that it requires sacrifice. We have tried to expose the challenges that a servant faces while, at the same time, trying to encourage our readers to get committed. If you do, you will make a difference; probably much more than you would expect. In addition, there are blessings that you wouldn't have even expected at all. Laura Story had a song that says it all: "…what if blessings come through raindrops? What if healing comes through tears? What if a thousand sleepless nights is what it takes to know You're near? What if trials of this life are Your mercies in disguise?"

So, here we are. It's time to make a decision. Are you going to persevere or just let this run off your back (missing the blessings that come with the rain)? Both of us know that getting involved, not committed, has been the right choice for us. Not every rain shower contains blessings, but something is blessed by the rain, even if we don't know it. The frustration for us has been seeing needs that can be filled by others that just get ignored. We know that we can't do everything, and we know that there is someone to whom God has laid out this opportunity. Sitting on the balcony only lets you see what you have missed.

Social entrepreneurship is more than just getting involved. Involvement may give you that *good feeling*, but feelings can rob you of the satisfaction of knowing you made a real difference. One of the talks on

Walk to Emmaus weekends is: Changing Our World. It is amazing to hear the things that the speakers have done in the name of Christ and how much difference they are making. They are heroes, but they don't go around claiming it. They have the satisfaction of hearing one day: "Well done, My good and faithful servant."

Profit was about how to get involved; *Service* is about committing yourself to a cause much greater than yourself. There are many ways to make a difference. Some of them are one-on-one, and the relationships that are formed in those settings is a wonderful thing. However, this book has mainly to do with entrepreneurship – specifically, social entrepreneurship. We have spoken about it in scattered statements throughout the book, but now we want to end with an explanation and a challenge.

Most entrepreneurs are always on the lookout for a need and/or opportunity. It was not a large leap for us to see the value of social entrepreneurship. Consider the following:

"Give a man a fish, and he'll eat for a day. Teach a man to fish, and he'll eat for a lifetime. Give him ownership of the pond, and his community will eat." Shawn Duncan, the Lupton Center.

For-profit or Non-profit?

We realize that some of our readers haven't been bitten by the *entrepreneur bug*. The most important thing about this is that being a part of a project that focuses on social entrepreneurship means you buy into the concept. There is some pushback from many who don't feel that using non-profit funding to help forprofit enterprises is appropriate. Let's look at what has been said over the course of this book. Lack of necessary funding, adversarial attitudes by lenders and others, inadequate preparation for taking on such a challenge, and other impediments stand in the way of potential entrepreneurs getting a successful venture going. These things all scream out for parties that are not a part of the project itself (in other words, don't have a dog in the fight) to join in the effort to solve the problem. This is what Luke 16 Corp is all about recruiting want-to-be entrepreneurs to be mentored and groomed for success.

Objectives - The differences between for-profit and nonprofits are reflected by the language they use to help identify what they stand for. Profits, revenues, and increases in stock prices reflect the key items for for-profit businesses. Social entrepreneurs, on the other hand, are focused on what benefits our society. Some of these would be broad social, cultural, and environmental. These seem to be in direct conflict with forprofits, but they don't have to be. Looking at areas such as poverty alleviation, health care, and community, one might see them as being more focused on social concerns. Our contention is that whatever affects the community at large affects all of the members of it in one way or the other.

Creation of Wealth - Some of the other concerns about social entrepreneurs have to do with the perceived lack of knowledge about the creation of wealth and being too narrowly focused on hot-button issues. There are cases of this, without a doubt. However, it would be like *throwing the baby out with the bathwater* to say that these instances permeate the landscape of non-profit businesses. In fact, social entrepreneurship is also made up of for-profits as well, and there are some hybrid situations. Some also say that these entrepreneurs focus on problems that don't currently exist. That is actually more of a slam on entrepreneurs in general, and it is not universally true.

Why Be a Non-profit? - Nathan never wanted to become a nonprofit because they get a bad rap anyway. Many causes that are championed by non-profits are absurd. The reason for the interest was two-fold: there are many very good projects that are supported only by grants, and social entrepreneurs are not all the same. Luke 16 Corp is one of the *hybrids* that exist to support for-profits except in one case. There are others on the drawing board, but they are not really part of Luke 16's primary mission. They support the community in very traditional ways, and only non-profits are awarded these grants.

Here is how this type operates: for-profit businesses can be supported by non-profits under certain circumstances. The key to this is to make sure that the non-profit is not creating a gain not invested somewhere else. Additionally, they aren't supposed to be in competition with other similar businesses. They are to contribute to the strengthening of the community at large. Benefit corporations (or B corps) are for-profits that ostensibly operate as if they were non-profit, but they don't have specific tax advantages. But for the ability to secure grants earmarked for non-profits, the B Corp makes a lot of sense if you want to be a for- profit with the goal of being a great citizen. One of the aspects of being a non-profit social entrepreneur is that it can also be a lending institution. There are loans made available for small businesses through the U.S. Department of Agriculture (USDA). It is another benefit of social entrepreneurship. The rates are really good and can be coupled with a grant. The USDA also offers great deals for residential single-family and multi-family construction projects as well. This adds to the number of items that they can offer to assist in community development.

Probably the most important aspect to Luke 16 Corp is that a 501(c)3 non-profit can apply for grants that offer the local community the opportunity to take on projects that will benefit the citizens without trying to get a corporation to support it. Examples would be recycling and community beautification. At the same time, they can help strengthen entrepreneurial efforts to create for-profit businesses in order to address gaps in retail categories, which would help attract more business to certain locales. These can also be done by taxing certain areas to raise funds for construction, but social entrepreneurs can accomplish the same thing without increasing taxes to local citizens. Sometimes it makes it hard for non-residents to justify shopping in such locations.

What About Community Development? - For us, helping people get into and to succeed in business is very gratifying. When young adults want to move back to many rural towns and cities, there aren't many jobs for them. The school districts in many of these areas are the largest employers. Unfortunately, that can become inbred, and there are some very qualified people who aren't able to find a good job in order to live in and support the community. If there isn't anything to keep teachers when they retire and/or their children graduate, they often leave the area. While their jobs become vacant, the desire of moving to an area with a declining population just isn't there for those from outside of it.

The best way for this to help is to have local citizens take up the challenge of revitalizing the community. If others come to do construction work or other tasks, they are not going to have the drive to stay with the projects until completion – or to help make them lasting. Then there is the matter of local jobs being done by outsiders. After all, the object is to strengthen the community, not just reconstruct it.

Are There Other Alternatives?

As we have been involved with mission-type projects in various areas, we have seen groups that come to help in rebuilding communities. There are some that actually set up a center from which to operate. World Vision is very active in some community efforts, and there are others that are locationspecific or operate in certain regions. There are even some organizations similar to Luke 16 Corp. Some investigation in the area where you are located should reveal who these are. Getting involved with an existing organization could be just the ticket. You might be able to add some other ministries that are not currently in place. It would be our pleasure to be able to assist in any way that makes sense for both parties.

Social Enterprises – It may be cutting the line rather finely to make a further distinction, but we believe that it is worth addressing. Basically, if for-profit businesses are going to be the outcome of the project, it is probably true social entrepreneurship. As noted earlier, this type of organization can, itself, be either a for-profit or non-profit. When a *social enterprise* is the structure of the organization, it is the basis of the project itself. An example might be a company that conducts mission trips that focus on doing good for communities and charges participants. Other than overhead, the amounts that are received go directly to the cost of travel and materials used on the various projects. There is no real economic benefit to the local communities. There are many like this, and the difference is whether there is an impact from the standpoint of economic development.

Social Businesses - Additionally, there are investors who can have an impact on local economies without being either of these social structures. Many would-be start-ups need capital to get their idea put into reality. Regardless of how this happens, the impact will be on the community both from the standpoint of the entrepreneurs and the people who have jobs because of them. As noted earlier, organizations can provide the fuel (cash) to help make the launch possible. Nonprofits can do this through the means of grants or low-cost loans, but *social businesses* can do this directly as any standard lending institution would. The benefit of this is that it is a revolving loan fund whose funds do not come from donations. Profit is not their motive, and they participate in building churches, mosques, art museums, community centers, and the like.

Education - There are quite a few organizations that train entrepreneurs. These are typically more like mentoring organizations in that there is more involvement in the success of the business. Beyond strictly training the entrepreneur, site location, funding sources, legal matters, marketing, and accounting may be a part of their offering.

Research - Some organizations, mostly non-profits, engage in research activities to assist in various community-building activities. These can be very beneficial to individuals and companies that need solid data to assist them in their quest for the development and funding of projects related to communities. They may focus on a geographical area or perhaps an industry. It has been our experience that start-ups or businesses/organizations seeking to expand find these services to be invaluable to their needs.

While this has provided some insight into the world of missionoriented entrepreneurship, there are a lot of different approaches to the matter. Our interest in the social entrepreneurship concept has to do with the ability to help in a holistic way so that entrepreneurs are not bouncing around trying to get help and support for their businesses. Additionally, there are few organizations that seek to build community as a part of these efforts. We would be pleased to assist existing ministries or those that would like to consider starting something of this sort.

Appendix D offers some opportunities that might be of interest to you.

Are You Ready?

Hopefully, you have become very interested in some of the things we have put forth. Now may not be the time to *pull the trigger*, but you shouldn't put this on the shelf to review it at a later time. Timing is everything, for sure, but it is so easy to let this go. Our experience has been that you shouldn't let a day go by that you don't do something to help you get closer to making a decision. Your decision may be that this is not what you want to take on. That's OK, but remember the assessment you did on spiritual gifts. If you work through that again, you should know whether it is right for you or not.

Prayer is the best thing that you can do, but you can also run this by people whose opinions you trust. If they are really the kind of friend you need, they will give you an honest answer. There are people that will be affirming because they don't want to let you down. There are those who may be jealous, or maybe they are just the overly cautious type. Make sure you are honest about what you have found and what you feel. If this process doesn't reveal a clear answer, you probably need to do more research. We have found that God will put clues in your path if you are open to Him. Satan will put things out there too, so be cautious about the ones that seem too good to be true.

We have mentioned some organizations, and there are many more. Your church should have some that they recommend as well. If you aren't connected with a church, you can reach out to us. We will do our best to get you in touch with some folks that can help you. If you can't find something that fits you, maybe you should start something yourself. If you do, be careful to try to model an existing group or organization to the maximum that it fits your situation.

After starting Luke 16 Corp, Nathan sought out coffee shop formats that might be applicable to the area. The experience of working with Sam Malek, founder of More Than Coffee in St. Louis, was amazing. What a wonderful soul Sam is, and he doesn't let his physical impairments get him down. Unfortunately, the area we were in is not like St. Louis in so many ways. Sam was very affirming, but he had to admit that his format just wasn't for us. If we had been earlier in our existence, we might have bailed on it. God knows better than we do, and He worked a scenario that fit us much better. It has been tough in many ways – we have shared much of that with you. While there are many things we would like to have changed, every challenge is an opportunity. We have witnessed God acting in amazing ways as we struggled through the early stages. In the end, there will be other challenges, and the ministry may not have a long run. That's up to God, and we honor whatever He has in store.

The Challenge

The book has provided a lot of information. Much of it may have been foreign to you. Our goal has been to broaden your horizons. This can be very liberating and a bit scary at the same time. It is our desire for your eyes to have been opened as Casting Crowns described in their awesome song - *Jesus, Friend of Sinners:*

> *Oh Jesus, friend of sinners*
> *Open our eyes to the world at the end of our pointing fingers.*
> *Let our hearts be led by mercy.*
> *Help us reach with open hearts and open doors.*
> *Oh Jesus, friend of sinners, break our hearts for what breaks yours.*

The world doesn't have to be far away, it can be "at the end of our pointing fingers". To quote Lily Tomlin:

"I said, "Somebody should do something about that." Then I realized I am somebody."

Of course, that doesn't mean that you should take on the world's problems by yourself. We had you do a Spiritual Gifts assessment so you could get yourself directed properly. Yogi Berra is credited with saying: "It is amazing what you can see if you look." The song above asks Jesus to "open our eyes". Jesus said: "This is why I speak to them in parables: 'Though seeing, they do not see; though hearing, they do not hear or understand.' We believe that God provides opportunities to us all the time. They are everywhere around us. Whether we see them or not depends on having our eyes opened to them by the Holy Spirit. Through prayer and enlightened awareness, we can be able to respond to the calling that has been placed on us.

Responding as a servant makes our task much easier. Knowing that God is already working and using prayer to help us see where and how to get involved, means that we can find our purpose and live it out. This is the assurance that we are serving in the way in which we have been prepared.

CONCLUSION

Maybe a better title for this chapter would be: CONCLUSIONS. That's not a normal form, so we can leave it like it is. Our reasoning is: it really is the beginning for you. You have been acquainted with what service is and how to effectively be in service to others. We have asked you to do a Spiritual Gifts assessment to learn how you are wired by our Creator to be in service. If you were not energized by the process at that point, maybe we didn't do the job we needed to for that to happen.

Maybe it was not enough for you to just be *informed*. That's natural. Maybe it's just that you weren't at the right point to realize what you have been missing. We need to be ready in order to begin to feel the passion of living out how we were designed to be. Timing is everything, and perhaps it just wasn't right for you. If that is the case, we hope you won't give up on the idea. You can still profit from the *Opportunities* section in Appendix D. That should help you be aware of signals you will be receiving if you are sincerely seeking fulfillment.

On the other hand, if you are intrigued by the possibilities that await you, welcome to the wonderful world of enlightenment. Well, that might not be the right term, but hopefully, you are seeing things more clearly. Taking the next steps is vital for you to keep heading in the right direction. Your pace may be slower or faster than others. Remember, timing is still a part of your reaching the heights that God has for you.

Be sure to carefully discern your place in the bigger scheme of things. Gifting and talent are not necessarily the same. Your vocation may be different as well. Both of us were in the world of work for many years before we settled on things that matter to us. In Jeff's case, he has married several things into a career with many facets. If that happens to you, you may have joined those of us who like to keep a lot of balls up in the air. In Nathan's case, God needed to have some detours along the way that prepared him to mentor entrepreneurs in many aspects and fields of endeavor. Don't worry; he's not going into brain surgery.

We want you to be aware of how the book may not be your primary *modus operandi*. Service, as you should know by now, has many facets. Your future may not be as an entrepreneur. However, you could very well support entrepreneurial ventures or projects in other ways than leading the pack. That's certainly important since lenders and others shy away from riskier projects. One of the great things about working as a group (hopefully a community) is that you form relationships that matter.

The first line of *The Purpose-Driven Life* by Rick Warren is: "It's not about you." That turns off some people because they believe that it is about them. Nathan always says that if it's about you, it's not about God

– and vice versa. On the other hand, here, it may be about God, you, and the person(s) you are serving. When you do what you are called to do, you will be giving the glory to God. Also, you will be blessed as a faithful servant.

Important Points to Remember

There are many well-intended ministries available. The preponderance of them is in the mode of the traditional mission work format. Many people have had their *dignity* taken away from them by those who feel that they are doing the right thing. It is a sad reality that we must face, but we can provide a better way.

While the ultimate outcome is up to God, we are to be faithful to the part that we are to play in the process. We cannot control what happens if people do not decide to follow the guidance that came from your involvement. If you have been truly faithful, God will honor that. In Acts 2:47, we are told that God added daily to those being saved.

Ultimately, we are asking that your goal be to help restore dignity to the folks who have had it taken away through means that are misguided.

We must guard against those actions that would further perpetuate the problem. Some powerful ways have been provided to involve both the servant and the one being served to achieve the greatest possible outcomes. Many times, it doesn't come like a bolt of lightning, but it can have the same powerful effect when done properly.

Please let us know how we can help. Our contact info is in Appendix D. We would also love to know if we have been able to help you get directed as a servant leader. As with all that we do in this valuable project, we live to make service a major part of how we live our lives.

May the Spirit go with you.

Afterword

As this was being written, the pandemic known as COVID-19 has been ravaging the world. The number of people who have been diagnosed as having been infected is rising rapidly as each day passes. There are suspicions surrounding the source itself and how it has been spread. We may never know the truth about all of this. It seems fitting, given the nature of this book, that we should look at the reactions of the populations as they struggle to seek a remedy and discover how to vaccinate those who aren't yet infected.

To our knowledge, no one is alive that has witnessed the magnitude of this disease. Even with our sophisticated methods of healing, we seem so woefully inept as we seek solutions. However, as it always is, this is an opportunity to see God's hands at work here. What we are able to see is, for the most part, quite extraordinary. In the U.S., the events of September 11, 2001, will always be remembered as a time when the country came together as we tried to make sense of what we had witnessed. Beginning with the first responders at the Twin Towers, people stepped up to help address the needs that were created by the events of that day and beyond.

While this pandemic will possibly go on for a long time yet, the American spirit is far from being broken. The signs of the country coming together are amazing to behold. For the most part, asking people to stay home for an indefinite time has brought the desired responses. The Congress appropriated an amazing sum of money to be able to assist virtually every person to make it through the crisis without becoming destitute.

Of course, we don't know how effective all of this will be, but we do know that the outpouring of support has been remarkable.

Here are some of the actions that have been taken so far:

- Distilleries went from producing liquor to making hand sanitizer.

- Medical personnel put their lives on the line in a way that only rivals wartime.

- Rice University came up with a respirator that can be created quickly and at a small fraction of the cost of the larger one.

- Auto manufacturers started making respirators, and some of these will be exported to other countries who haven't the capability to make the rapid change-over themselves.

- A Fox News weatherman has created a company to make rainwear and is now able to make face masks in large quantities.

- Delivery services and drivers stepped up to help deliver meals and other necessities to those who are unable to get out themselves. Companies that normally do deliveries have greatly increased their driver crews.

- Churches, schools, and other organizations that normally have large groups assembled have converted their worship and other services, teaching, etc., to an online format.

- Sales of patriotic items have sky-rocketed.

- Restaurants and retailers offered curbside service to cut down on the amount of traffic inside a business.

- Schools have had many obstacles to overcome, but they have adapted much better than would have been expected.

On the other hand, there were some very negative actions as well:

- Politics showed its ugly side in bogus debates about things that really didn't have anything to do with the situation. Mostly, these were efforts to get funding for things that were not related.

- Some municipalities restricted churches from having any type of gatherings. Unfortunately, some pastors didn't help by their actions, either.

- Some governors didn't seem to get that the economy has been in free fall since the beginning of the pandemic. Restrictions on opening many businesses were onerous and over-the-top.

- A lot of finger-pointing only slowed the assistance to citizens, and some businesses were unfairly given stimulus funding.

- The rush to flood the economy with "free" money from the government has caused all sorts of problems. Laidoff workers were encouraged to stay off the job because benefits for being unemployed exceeded their regular pay. Now, cries for universal pay without working are fueling the desire of citizens to vote for those who would pay them for *breathing*. The plan is to give this to undocumented aliens as well!

- States and businesses that were struggling before the pandemic are, in some cases, trying to get well at the taxpayers' expense.

- Suicides have likely spiked due to the virus. The pandemic is pushing mental health issues to crisis levels. Clinics that deal with them have not functioned at normal levels since the start of the crisis.

- Unfortunately, there are some industries that will have a long slog ahead of them. Airlines, hotels, convention centers, and others that have difficulty keeping social distance are struggling with how to adapt to the changes they must make.

It has been said that those who refuse to consider history are doomed to repeat it. Sadly, this truth haunts us now and will haunt us in the future.

The Good News

We would not be true to our purpose if we ended this book with bad news. However, it is very important to learn from our mistakes; failures need to be strongly considered so we can improve. It seems quite a daunting task sometimes, given the amount of change that keeps coming at us these days. This is why it is our duty to focus on the things that we can change and not get hung up on global issues that are out of our control anyway.

Elie Wiesel, Holocaust survivor and Nobel Laureate, said, "The opposite of love is not hate, it's indifference." You could also say that it is *apathy*, as Nathan did in *Profit*. The point is the same and echoes the Casting Crowns song cited in Chapter 9.

It is our belief that, by addressing the problems we have with regard to serving others, we can begin to build relationships that help us to create a sense of community. When we are looking out for each other, we not only lift them up, but we are lifted up ourselves.

APPENDIX A

Tribalism

There are still places in the world where cultures are divided into tribes, much like they have been from almost the beginning of time. Even animals tend to gather in tribal-like packs. We are gregarious people, for the most part, but most of us aren't comfortable in crowds. Loneliness is a big problem today, and it is amazing considering how many people there are on earth. Communication is amazing, but we don't seem to know very much. That is most likely due to what Ronald Reagan was conveying when he said: "It is not that they are ignorant; it is just that they know so much that is not true." All of this tends to create a situation like the one we have currently: people banding together in groups in order to get what they want or to preserve their way of life.

Tribes tend to have something that naturally connects them. They may be related to each other, but this only goes so far since incest leads to its own set of problems. When the Israelites were taken into exile by their enemies, God warned them about intermarriage with their captors. Like most warnings, there were lots of people who didn't heed it. There are religions that seek to prohibit marriage outside of their faith. If you are Protestant, you share that distinction with over 300 denominations. Each denomination has something that differentiates it from the others. Some are more restrictive than others about marrying a person of another denomination. Islam and Judaism are generally more restrictive in that regard, but much of that has to do with how strong a person is about adhering to those and other restrictions.

What we seem to have more of today is "clannish" groups. They are quite "tribal" in nature in that they seem to have the same characteristics regarding how they become a group (however it is composed). The ones that become more of a concern are generally known as *cults*. What makes this so is that cults normally have rules and conditions that are outside of the mainstream, and they require "allegiance" to their basic tenets. Most of these groups do not seem to want to be called cults; I would expect that is because some of the things they do are illegal.

It has always been puzzling to us as to why some of the groups form in the first place. Further, it has been equally amazing how their leaders were chosen. In Biblical times, the choice came from family hierarchical processes leading to a succession within the family. Middle to far Eastern cultures and American Indians seem to have used some sort of contests involving physical skills centered on fighting. Elections were first used by Greeks and Romans around the time of Christ's time on earth. Still, the "divine right of kings" was and still is in force. However, it was communicated, these leaders called upon the blessing of God or some other sort of deity to support their notion that they were to lead their people. Elections led to political parties who held differing opinions on matters affecting their constituencies. Some tribes voted on important matters, but even the dictators of today are pretty much autocrats. Malcolm Gladwell, author of *The Tipping Point*, described many brains, by exclusion, that have little capacity for connecting with a large portion of the population. Neurologists suggest that this is why tribalism is an inescapable fact of society. Once these brains have reached their capacity to make connections with others, they have to devise some sort of scheme to keep track of them.

Dr. John MacArthur, in *Joy Rules*, points out that the Greek word for love in Philippians 1:9 is *agape*. Here, Paul writes: "It is my prayer that your love may abound more and more, with knowledge and all discernment" (ESV). Here's how he sees this: "It is decisive love – the word agapē means the love of the will, or the love of choice, not emotion. It is dynamic love; it abounds more and more, increasing and overflowing. It is deep love, in that it is rooted in deep spiritual knowledge and understanding. And it is discerning love, in that it has insight into all the situations of life and knows how it should be applied." So, he describes a scenario where a group starts out with a fellowship that they believe to be agape. Later, they become drawn into *nepotism* (only family) or *cronyism* (only friends). Discerning love is no longer a part of it. They become inwardly focused on the exclusion of outsiders.

The U.S. found out in Afghanistan that dealing with all the tribes made it difficult to come to a collective moral. So, what exists is a delicate balance being maintained by the government of the country. When some of the tribes moved away from that and supported the Taliban, a group of tribes formed the Northern Alliance. This had the support of the U.S. and other nations who opposed the Taliban. Once we invaded the country and sought to restore a democratic government, we found just how difficult it is to try to get all of these tribes on the same page.

It is our feeling that dealing with large urban areas is much the same as dealing with a country like Afghanistan. There are groupings that might approximate the nature of tribes, and some of the most significant ones are gangs of mainly ethnic young people. During the "Black Lives Matter" period, the U.S. has seen protests that exhibit the control that these groups can exert on an otherwise peaceful populace. It's hard to know what makes some gangs form and become so violent. The "Crips" and the "Bloods" are two that seem to always be in contention with each other in cities. Their roots date back to the years after WWII when racial segregation and poverty led young black men to form into groups. While there were territorial considerations, there were financial issues as well.

It seems that organized crime fits the model of tribes in many ways. Mostly, they were referred to as "families". They were essentially the same ethnic groups, although that changed in the years following the Prohibition era structures. Most of their focus was on engaging in activities that brought them wealth by illicit means. They were quite violent, and "gang wars" broke out on a fairly frequent basis. It has always amazed me to hear of the pervasiveness of their involvement in various industries. A former "Mafia don" said that the "mob" infiltrated the unions in order to worm their way into the industries that the unions represented.

There is a common bond for people to be drawn to when they face misery (perceived or real). Organizers or leaders that can communicate effectively can use this to build their ranks. There is also arrogance in success that causes people to not be as attentive to constituents as should be the case. What I am referring to is how these "tribal" groups reach the point of being successful enough that they aren't necessarily concerned about recruiting more members.

The Nazis in World War II showed how powerful propaganda can be. It seems that it has been this way throughout history. People tend to ignore the sources that they feel are not telling them the straight story. What happens in the U.S. today is that "trusted" news sources are aligned politically, and there is far too much opinion included in what is purported to be news. News people mostly want to report something controversial, so they are quick to jump on a story that would further inflame the passions of the competitors. Some people like good news, but mostly people seem to want something that is tantalizing. Otherwise, our news sources wouldn't be full of that stuff. The point is that all of this is pandering to some group. We tend to become synthesized to those things that are directed to us. This is so insidious and so pervasive that we hardly know that it is going on. Now, this is not universally true, but let's say you have an affinity for an athletic team. The team could be from a school that you went to or whatever. They call people who support such teams "fans." (short for "fanatics"). It's amazing that people can get so passionate about things that really don't matter. The only thing that makes sense is that being a part of a group enables us to live vicariously through the group. But that is why we follow celebrities, isn't it? Probably one of the reasons it is true is due to what the philosopher Goethe was describing when he said that we are smart as individuals but ignorant as a crowd.

Think about how different it would be if you were part of a group that actually did something meaningful. Of course, I mean something more than sitting around and commiserating with each other or complaining about the price of eggs (oh, we don't do that anymore, do we?) or whatever. What a difference it could make to be a part of something bigger than yourself; something that makes a difference. Focusing on results is what makes the difference, and being a part of a group that has that mindset is how you can have it.

Who is calling the shots for you? Are you being led by a "tribal leader", someone who has risen to the top of the heap by rather draconian methods? Have you risen by hard work and then been elected/chosen to be the leader? What kind of group are you in? Do you just sort of go along with the crowd? What drives you to do what you do?

The answers to these questions will have a tremendous bearing on how successful you can be at creating a healthy community that has the potential to be successful.

APPENDIX B

L.a.L.a. Land

There was a movie by this name that won several Oscars in 2017. Along with the name of the city (Los Angeles), the title describes a place where we often feel that we are, and it is generally thought that this is where people just "don't get it". We're not sure where this came from, but I made an acrostic that fits the concept:

(L)ethargic

(A)pathetic

(L) ackadaisical

(A)nti-capitalisitic

Not all of these are present in every situation, but it can be enough for only one to be a part of the mix. We will look at each of these and see what the impact can be of having one or more of them as an ingredient of the mindset of the residents.

LETHARGIC

Merriam-Webster's definition of the word lethargy includes the quality or state of being lazy, sluggish, or indifferent. Some synonyms are: languor and stupor. These suggest that there is inertia or listlessness from either internal or external sources. Depression is one of the most common illnesses that contributes to the condition. The external forces can be just as pervasive. There are a whole host of antonyms that illustrate how much of a problem this can be: eagerness, enthusiasm, keenness, spiritedness, ambition, enterprise, vim, vigor, and vitality.

These are words that can be used to describe passion. So, it is logical to believe that lethargy is a lack of passion. Dr. Phil McGraw says that passion is what gets you up in the morning.

People, by nature, tend to get comfortable with things they know. This is true even if the situation they find themselves in is less than optimum. Part of it is probably due to the fact that there is a fear of the unknown, and change is not high on the list of desirability. Regardless of the reason, making progress depends on a willingness to take on something new or different.

Philip Crosby provided his Theory of Human Behavior: People subconsciously retard their own intellectual growth. "They rely on clichés and habits. Once they reach the age of their own personal comfort with the world, they stop learning, and their mind runs idle for the rest of their days. They may progress organizationally, they may be ambitious and eager, and they may even work night and day. But they learn no more." Admittedly, this is a rather bleak assessment; however, the point is a critical one. This seems to be more prevalent in bureaucratic scenarios. The military is a prime example of the extent to which this can go. There are regulations for virtually everything, and those in charge are responsible for ensuring complete adherence to these. The need to very strictly "follow the rules" is fairly obvious in such situations. The unfortunate thing is that people get so fixed on the rules and regulations that they don't do a very good job of thinking. Most governmental agencies lean heavily on them, and it slows the operation immensely.

The paradox is that, as a pilot, you are, on the one hand, absolutely required to know what to do when operating an aircraft, while on the other hand, there is a lot that has to be done in case of emergencies. Basically, in the first case, you must do things without thinking, and in the second case, you must be able to react instinctively. While there is some flexibility in the process, for the most part, everything is expected to follow guidelines. The problem comes when people higher up the "totem pole" get so fixated on rules and regulations that operations become stagnated.

There are lots of experiences that we could relate, and readers probably have many as well. The effect this has on communities trying to secure funding for projects from governmental agencies or even private foundations is to squash initiative. The benefit mentioned earlier from the breach of a dam has been almost imperceptible due to the process being slow in distributing the funds and the lack of interest in rebuilding by most of the businesses that had been affected. Couple that with the endemic poverty and dependency on public assistance, and you will find a population that generally has little or no interest in changing things.

APATHETIC

It has been said that the opposite of *love* is not *hate,* it is *greed.* The encounter Jesus had with the rich ruler in Mark 10:17-31 shows that having *everything* tends to make one greedy, but, to us, greed at least leads to *apathy.* However, the rich themselves are not the only ones that can be apathetic about those in need. James 2:2- 7 tells of how partiality is shown in preferential treatment, and the poor get shoved aside. On the other hand, in verse 5, James specifically says that God has chosen the poor to be rich in faith and heirs of the Kingdom. Lest we be unkind to those who are very philanthropic, many wealthy people give much of their wealth and even of themselves.

In His Steps by Charles Sheldon was the beginning of WWJD – what would Jesus do? It is a fictitious account of a church in an inner-city location that had to be awakened to the poverty and injustice around them. Most of the members really weren't "bad" people; they just weren't paying attention to the world around them. Perhaps God sends us opportunities to increase our awareness of the needs that may be just outside our doors – figuratively speaking. The challenge we have is paying attention and then acting appropriately. We'll deal with that in another section, but overcoming our inertia is where we are called to act.

The first line of Rick Warren's *Purpose Driven Life* is: "It's not about you." Most of the book speaks of how we need to put ourselves in a lesser position, as a servant, as Jesus put it. Apathy doesn't have a direct connection to selfishness, but my guess is that being self-absorbed makes us less likely to be concerned about others.

LACKADAISICAL

OK, this may be close to *lethargic, but* there weren't any other "L" words that would fit. There is a difference – albeit a fine one. In a narrow definition, *lackadaisical* means "Lacking enthusiasm and determination; carelessly lazy". Whereas *lethargy* suggests that a person is just practically devoid of energy, we see *lackadaisical* as being at a different level with energy but without any drive or direction. This seems to be just sort of floating along, letting life take you where it will go. It may not be a problem to be a trash collector and let a little bit of trash fall out when emptying the can. On the other hand, if you are working with precision tolerances, being lackadaisical can lead to disastrous results.

It's not just being careless and lacking determination; the enthusiasm gap can cause a person to miss a lot of opportunities. It seems to us that lethargy can come from a lack of passion about much of anything. Being lackadaisical suggests that change is perhaps out of the realm of interest. Where this comes into play in community development projects is in whether you can expect folks to be interested in much of anything vs. doing something new and different that could lead to improvement.

What we have observed is a sort of plateauing effect where there is no interest in advancement. One way to describe such people is that they are "settlers". It's pretty easy to see how this fits: folks just seem to become satisfied with things the way they are. The man that Jesus encountered by the pool at Bethesda must have become somewhat satisfied. After all, he had been sitting by the pool for 38 years and hadn't been healed. That's an example of perseverance, but it gets worse. When Jesus asked the man if he wanted to be well, he gave the excuse that no one had carried him to the pool. The man obviously did want to be made well; Jesus healed him on the spot. If Jesus had carried him to the pool, the message would have been that the legend was true.

Kenneth Bailey spoke on Christian radio regarding matters such as this. He was the author of a book, *Jesus Through Middle Eastern Eyes,* and said that it was actually a job that some people had to be beggars. According to him, Jews were obliged to give alms to the poor, and particularly blind people were accepting their handouts to help them fulfill that.

So maybe the difference here is that lackadaisical is probably better defined as "intellectual laziness". It seems that a lot of people just don't think very deeply about things. They just accept things that make sense without doing any research. Wrong notions can be entrenched that way, and it is difficult to get through to them with a valid argument.

An example of this in rural communities is the fact that they are very protective of the land that they own. Additionally, they generally don't want their neighbors to sell the land they own either. It may be that they are concerned that land will be taken out of farm production. It probably means that there would be a lot of new folks around, crowding them in the stores and common areas. What they don't realize is that, in many cases, the largest demographic- and the only one that is growing – is adults 65 years old and over. Every citizen feels the impact of this, whether they know it or not. It is the decline of the capital base, which is not supporting services and not attracting new residents out of concern for property values declining further.

ANTI-CAPITALISTIC

The Presidential election of 2016 was an interesting time in a myriad of ways – understatement of the century. From time to time there have been business people who have served in political office, but the presidency has been one that has not drawn the right mix of peoples' desires and qualified candidates. There have been military leaders who have made it, but it was understandable in a time when there were struggles for power around the world that the U.S. had some interest in. With a country that is over $20 trillion in debt and coming off eight years of a president where there was 2% growth or less, people have recognized the need for someone to lead the country that knows how to make good business decisions. The unfortunate reality is that those who didn't support the ultimate decision on who would be president had a lot of trouble accepting the fact that there was tremendous discontent in the land.

The problem with characterizing a particular area as being *anti-capitalistic* is that it is a very pervasive attitude in the U.S. Perhaps we shouldn't come down too hard on this condition because it is so common. The point is that we have slowly let an anti-capitalistic mentality creep up on us. Early in the 20th century, John Maynard Keynes came up with a theory that became almost "gospel" to many economists and politicians. It has led to a strong leaning toward a reliance on government for far too many things.

The major problem with the anti-capitalistic mentality is that, since it essentially started with the movement toward socialism, the real growth is now with the people that espouse socialistic views. Also, since entrepreneurship is not in great favor with socialists, small business growth is hampered by the expansion of socialist ideals. How is it that folks like Mark Zuckerberg, the Facebook founder and CEO, are pushing the idea of a minimum income for all citizens? They wouldn't have to do anything to get it, but they can work if they want to. Zuckerberg says that this would free up entrepreneurs to be creative without being concerned with setbacks. One concept is that innovators can create robots to do all the work while they enjoy the benefits of their creations. I'm just not sure how this works. One viewpoint is: "Sloth has become sexy." That means we don't have to worry about defending our way of life because it won't be defensible if we don't have anything but robots to defend us – especially if they can be hacked into by our enemies.

This isn't a new concept, it turns out. There is a project going on in Finland that involves more than 20,000 people that receive the minimum income. Supposedly, Finland can't fill the available jobs, so they believe this will encourage people to work for more if they don't have the high welfare payments they are currently receiving. Huh?! It was shocking to hear that Thomas Paine wrote some of the same things in The Rights of Man. It wasn't shocking that President Franklin Roosevelt advocated it in a speech entitled *Freedom from Want.*

Ludwig von Mises gave a very interesting (and accurate) account of how socialism got its start. He goes back to the days of feudal times to describe the situation for the people who were artisans of the times. Basically, these people had no income except for being supported by royalty. The royals had pride in the quality of the work of these artisans. In those times, there was essentially no economic benefit to the kingdom from these artisans, and they were always "on the bubble" in terms of performing well enough to continue in the employ of the royalty. Nicolai Lenin seized on the fact that there were workers who were uneasy with the conditions of their working situation. This was coupled with the nonproduction workers who felt that they were due more for the contribution they made to the process. Entrepreneurialism was not encouraged and didn't really exist in such environments except in farming. It seems to me that governments (even those who "encourage" entrepreneurism) are more interested in having large corporations since they employ more people. Trade unions took the place of the sole proprietors in many industries. In this way, more control could be exerted by the sheer number of employees involved, and there was more at stake in retirement and unemployment funds.

Robert Lupton says that the world is awakening to the reality that healthy economic systems are fundamental to the elimination of poverty. You may have seen that we need a theological balance in our understanding of wealth. If some of the more resourced members of the wider church were to step forward, the church could see itself with a much broader role. Perhaps it could see itself as not just a purveyor of compassionate services but also a catalyst for fruitful economies. This could be the way to start bringing economic wholeness to struggling souls who have resigned to unending poverty for too long.

While the effects of this attitude are mostly felt at a higher level than in local communities, the way it manifests itself locally is in the individual's reliance on government "entitlements". So, the politicians create the programs to "benefit" those in need. On its face, these programs are necessary and truly help the recipients. Beneath the surface, however, much harm has been done through the dependency that results from such largess. How this trickles down from the initial benefit derived from the program has been addressed elsewhere.

Appendix C

Community

To most people, the word "community" probably brings up thoughts of a place, a location where some number of people live. If you live in a very small place, the town or hamlet that you live in may be referred to as a community. If you live in a large city, your idea of community may be only a block or two. Many times, we think of the areas in a city or large town as having neighborhoods rather than communities. The size of the area will obviously vary, but there is some definable grouping that determines how people connect with each other (or not!)

In larger cities like New York City, the notion of community takes on an entirely different connotation. It may only take a couple of blocks to encapsulate a neighborhood of residents who are of the same ethnicity. Many of them may work outside of the area, but their social life is generally within the boundaries of the neighborhood.

A similar situation also exists in suburbia. Many downtown areas are virtually empty or getting that way. Therefore, people tend to shop in stores near their homes if they provide the goods they purchase on a regular basis. This could be called "location loyalty," and it doesn't seem to be the case for products known as "shopping goods." These are the types that people don't purchase without giving consideration to the various differences among these products: quality, brand, price, selection and the like.

Rural areas tend to be somewhat like the suburbs. The problem there is that the shrinking economies are seeing most of the shops, services, etc., no longer available in the immediate area. In many areas in the western U.S. have been like this for some time, and people have either gotten accustomed to it or moved away. It's almost like watching dominos falling to see the effect of one smaller town after another being reduced to Dollar General stores and maybe a gas station or grocery store. Post offices are being centralized, and the services they render are going to local businesses as an add-on.

For sure a community is made up of different kinds of people. There is no such thing as homogeneity anymore when it comes to a group of people. Both of us have seen the decline precipitously occurring in the towns where we were born and grew up. Only the schools seem to hold the community together, but the children educated in them tend to move to find work when they graduate from high school.

This discourse is primarily intended to point out the importance of being a part of your community. There are many ways to do that, but being a person that people like is unfortunately not enough. You may be a member of the same church, be a regular participant in community activities/events, and be the kind of person people like to be around. These are all good things to do as a human being, and you can derive benefits from your being a good citizen. We have been in that position, and we have known a lot of business people who have as well.

What we want to impart in relation to the community is what can be done to support your community that shows you are concerned about it. This is where service comes into play. Churches, clubs, and athletic teams may be the best places to become a part of the community. You could run for public office, but politics doesn't make for any cohesiveness at all. Entrepreneurs can be some of the best at helping people to get interested in their community. Both of us have coached athletic teams. Nathan has been a leader in Boy Scouts in three different communities in which he lived. Churches offer another alternative, but some churches don't "play well with others". They become as competitive as athletic teams. It's hard to figure that one out.

Community members must look at how to work together to strengthen their community. Every part of their lives depends on it. Most people don't realize the significance of community because they are too focused on themselves. Schools, property values, and quality of life are all at stake. So are the safety and integrity of the citizens. We've seen the capital base become so eroded that people have to take major losses when they have to sell their homes. People don't want to buy because they know how hard it is to realize any sort of gain out of a sale when it comes time for them to relocate. Rental property loses value because the area attracts the wrong kind of renters. New housing is not built because the risk is just too high. There are programs available, but it takes a desire to get involved on more than just a personal level. It's not an easy process.

APPENDIX D

Opportunity

"We are defined by our opportunities; not just the ones that we take advantage of, but also by the ones we pass on."
Dale Earnhardt, Jr., an American race car driver

The notion of opportunity knocking seems to lack authenticity. It suggests that we are just sitting around one day, and a knock comes at the door. Our first option is to open the door or just ignore it. Depending on the choice, we either go on the journey of a lifetime or remain in couch potato mode. Our feeling is that God works better with a moving target. We are sure that there are times when He picks people out for special occasions, but we are all faced with opportunities around us as we go about our daily lives.

Nathan has had several experiences where he struggled over a decision to be made, and suddenly, the solution came in a flash. On the other hand, there have been lots of detours put in his path so that he could learn more about the matter first. When we answer a call in our lives, we are surrounded with opportunities to grow in faith and service. Our willingness to persevere (or not) will determine how extensive our participation in them will be.

The late motivational speaker and writer, Jim Rohn, used to make a point about getting started. It's about that being in motion thing. Remember the Chinese proverb that says: the journey of a thousand miles begins with one step. Growing in faith and action means that we must take responsibility for our own lives and explore how to be faithful to our calling. Become a recruiter of souls who need to be participants in becoming all that they can be.

Using questions in order to move things along

It was in the Preface that we first developed the idea that *questions* are important in being able to determine the nature of the challenge and the *Why?* That is: why would we want to take this on? A little later, we will cover the rest of the process, but we want to provide some suggestions at this point.

Nathan came across an article a while back that pointed out two words that can kill a project: What about? Many times, we get to the point of moving forward on a project when someone asks: "What about...?" Whatever the object (or should we say objection), the discussion can lead to all sorts of questions and objections that can derail the project. At a minimum, it can delay acting on an idea to the point where the window of opportunity closes.

Of course, one of the problems with being an entrepreneur or working with them is that they usually want to get on with the project – sometimes to the utter dismay of the other players. We advocate having a group approach to projects; that's where the *community* becomes involved. If you have laid the groundwork for that, you can begin to utilize the different gifts to create a holistic environment.

So, it's pretty important to get folks together to brainstorm about solving a problem. After all, that's really how we can make a difference. The idea of community pervades the entire process. If you aren't aware of it, let me say that it is pretty rough to act like a *lone ranger* when you are trying to accomplish something. Egos, attitudes, and downright stubbornness make life a real struggle. That is why we wrote earlier about getting to know the people you will be working with. It's not just that some people are contentious by nature; the *What about* matter often doesn't come from a good place.

What If Questions

Almost any substantive discussion or planning session is going to begin to falter at some point. Taking the process in a positive direction is critical to being fruitful and successful. Some people are better at guiding the process than others, but if we are sincere about it, we can all cultivate a spirit of optimism in such situations.

It has been our desire to lead you into a position of confidence when moving to the extremely important step of planning the direction you and your group will be taking. Asking *What-if* questions is what we believe is the key to effective planning at this juncture. It can be a springboard to a successful venture.

Here are some examples of how this can work. In your initial approach, you need to find ways to move people and resources where they are most useful and look for unmet needs and wants. As a long-time consultant working with small business owners, Nathan found that people mostly wanted to do something they liked and be able to make money in the process. However, most people don't have the skills to handle all the vagaries of carrying out their plans. If they are skilled in doing the actual work, they probably don't know how to do the other required tasks. If they are adept at managing a business operation, they may have just fallen in love with the notion of doing that kind of business. In either case, they will undoubtedly have a rough road ahead of them and perhaps not be successful.

Our experience has been that it is important to talk with as many people as you can about what it is that you want to do. OK, but you may be thinking that others will steal your ideas. You need confidentiality, for sure. That's very important, and we agree that you need to be careful who you talk with. There are other things that can come from your conversations, like *making friends*. Of course, they are not going to give you any great ideas, but you can greatly benefit from what they know about the industry you want to get involved in. In the end, however, you and your group must decide how to proceed.

The big point to be made here is to do as much research as you can, and you will get ideas that can be developed into a successful enterprise.

Don't be discouraged if things don't go as fast as you would like them to. The idea may take a lot of twists and turns along the way, and it may not look much like you thought it would. Both of us have spent lots of unproductive, frustrating time on projects that didn't work out very well. Learn all you can along the way, because it will serve well at some point. There really isn't any useless information, even if it means that you learn that you won't ever do that again. You will, of course, but there are always new things to experience.

Management By Wandering Around (MBWA) - This is notion by Earl Nightingale. The point made was that only you can learn about what is going on in your *domain* by getting out from behind your desk and taking a look around. A friend of Nathan's once told him that the best fertilizer for crops is the farm manager's footprints in the field. Even in the amazing world of communication and video images, we can't know what is happening like you can by "getting out into the field".

One of the reasons that we don't like bureaucracies is that they *pigeonhole* people into their cubicles or offices. An education administrator once told Nathan: "What you need to understand about a bureaucracy is that the best thing you can do is to avoid making waves." No wonder nothing gets done!

Sadly, when bureaucrats do get out of their comfort zone, they are so whacked out by the pressure that exists in their surroundings that all they want to do is to get away for a while. Don't think that we are against taking breaks; we all need that on a regular basis. However, *escapism* is normally the route that is taken instead. The point here is: finding real problems that are crying out for solutions requires opening your eyes *to the world at the end of our pointing fingers**.

Why Questions

You may find the *Why* jumping out at you before you determine the *What*. It's fine if that is the scenario. All situations are different, so the point is to get yourself pointed in the right direction. A famous quote attributed to President John Kennedy goes like this: "Some people look at things the way they are and ask 'Why?'. I look at things the way they could be and ask, 'Why not?'" In such cases, the *Why* may be a given.

You find yourself looking for ways to lead you to *Why not?* Questions. It takes courage to engage in a quest for solutions when the easy thing to do is to put up with the status quo.

If you are starting with *Why*, you must have some sense of the *What*. The things referred to by Kennedy are the *what* in that instance. This is getting a bit circular, but the point here is: these two go hand-in-hand. Let's see if we can make this a bit simpler:

> You walk down the street, and you see a woman crying (what). It is not apparent why, but you stop to consider it. If you can determine the reason (why), perhaps you can consider what to do about it. You then look at some possible solutions (how). As you work through the process of finding the best solution, you vet the options (what if). When the solution is selected, you still have more questions (how about). You should be able to then ask the final question: why not?

In the end, the important thing is that you go through some process like the one described above. You commit yourself to seeing it through and move toward a satisfactory outcome. There will probably be speed bumps along the way and perhaps, even some detours. Your willingness to persevere will make a major difference in how successful you will be.

Discovering Opportunities

In the realm of social entrepreneurship, there are some major areas where the kind of opportunities we've been referring to exist. Here are some suggestions:

1. Recycling – there are many opportunities, but some of them are crying out for social entrepreneurs. Luke 16 is currently looking at one in particular. Basically, the challenge is to find a way to efficiently get the refuse items to a place where it can be prepared for reduction to a shredded state. The process will then move through heating, molding, and finishing. At that point, it is suitable for re-entering the stream of commerce. We'll be announcing the outcome of our efforts in a few months.

2. Virtual incubators – the corporate partner will assist potential entrepreneurs to start and manage their businesses. There are various forms that this could take, but the aim is to truly prepare the owners to have a successful launch and be supported in meaningful ways. Ownership may be shared initially.

3. Contests – this is the recruiting of groups who will work together on a project. The framework of the business opportunity will be set forth, and the groups will compete for the awarding of the funding for the project. Some colleges are doing something similar to this, and those would be opportunities as well. Our aim is to be able to support the winning group long enough to have a successful launch and beyond.

What follows is a list of some of the resources/organizations that can provide more specific guidance on how to get on with your involvement. Most of these provided information that was helpful in writing this book. Now that you have a better handle on the direction you would like to take, you can be prepared to do your due diligence with some of these. Our experience has been that the more you delve into this, the more you will be led to. Be discerning. Some organizations have strong appeal, and not all of them are what they purport to be. We hope we have given you enough guidance to make solid judgments as you work through the process:

1. FCS Urban Ministries – The organization created by Robert Lupton – https://www.fcsministries.org

2. The Apparent Project – The Haitian project helping keep families together - https://apparentproject.org

3. Luke 16 Corp – The project in Iron County, MO, that Nathan is involved with – www.luke16.org - email: luke16corp@outlook.com - phone 1.888.360.5327 - mobile/text 417.270.0677

4. The Rainbow Network – Nicaragua - https://www.rainbownetwork.org

5. Cooperative Baptist Fellowship – Rural Development Coalition: Together for Hope - Cbf.net/missions

6. *When Helping Hurts: Alleviating Poverty Without Hurting the Poor.. . and Yourself.* Steve Corbett and Brian Fikkert 2009 Moody Publishers

7. *A Billion Bootstraps Microcredit, Barefoot Banking, and the Business Solution for Ending Poverty* by Phil Smith and Eric Thurman. New York: McGraw-Hill, 2007.

8. *How the Church Fails Businesspeople (and what can be done about it)* by John Knapp. Grand Rapids: William Eerdmans, 2012.

9. *Church on Sunday, Work on Monday: The Challenge of Fusing Christian Values with Business Life* by Laura Nash and Scotty McClennan. San Francisco, Jossey-Bass, 2001.

10. *The Soul of a Business: Managing for Profit and the Common Good* by Tom Chappell. New York: Bantam Books, 1994.

11. *The 3 Colors of Ministry* by Christian Schwarz. St. Charles, IL: ChurchSmart Resources, 2001.

12. *EntreLeadership: 20 Years of Practical Business Wisdom from the Trenches* by Dave Ramsey. New York: Howard Books, 2001.

13. Certified B Corporation – bcorporation.net - Certified B Corporations are businesses that meet the highest standards of verified social and environmental performance, public transparency, and legal accountability to balance profit and purpose. B Corps is accelerating a global culture shift to redefine success in business and build a more inclusive and sustainable economy.

14. Net Impact – netimpact.org - Net Impact inspires and equips emerging leaders to build a more just and sustainable world.

15. Stephen Ministries - Christ-centered care to hurting people. https://www.stephenministries.org/

REFERENCE LIST

Bailey, Kenneth. *Jesus Through Middle Easter Eyes,* InterVarsity Press 2008

Berra, Yogi. American professional baseball catcher, manager and coach and author.

Beaumont, Susan. *How to Lead When You Don't Know Where You're Going: Leading in a Liminal Season.* Lanham, MD: Rowman & Littlefield Publishers, 2019

Begg, Alistair. *Not So With You.* https://www.truthforlife.org/

Blanchard, Ken. *Servant Leadership* – LinkedIn course. the Chief Spiritual Officer of The Ken Blanchard Companies. Author of *The One Minute Manager* - William Morrow Co., 1982

Branson, Richard. business magnate, investor, author and former philanthropist.

Clifton, Jim. *The Coming Jobs War: What Every Leader Must Know About the Future of Job Creation.* New York: Gallup Press, 2011.

Collins, Jim. *Good to Great: Why Some Companies Make the Leap... and Others Don't.* Harper Collins, 2001.

Crosby, Phillip. Quality is Free, Penguin 1980

Cuban, Mark. American entrepreneur, television personality, media proprietor, and investor.

Delp, Katie. Executive Director, *FCS Urban Ministries.* Atlanta

Diamond, Amira, and Kramer, Melanie. Co-Founders of the Women's Earth Alliance

Diefenderfer, Rick. Director at Creating Christian Communities. Joshua, TX

Dodge, Mary Mapes. *The Little Red Hen.* 1874

Duncan, Shawn. Director of Training, *FCS Urban Ministries.* Atlanta Edison, Thomas. American inventor and businessman.

Ferguson, Dave and Warren Bird. *Hero Maker: Five Essential Practices for Leaders to Multiply Leaders.* Grand Rapids: Zondervan, 2018.

Gandhi, Mahatma. https://iheartintelligence.com/mostinspiring-quotes-mahatma-gandhi/

Gladwell, Malcolm. *The Tipping Point: How Little Things Can Make a Difference.* Little Brown, 2015.

Goleman, Daniel. *Why We Aren't More Compassionate.* TED Talk.

Hammett, Eddie. *Reaching People Under 30 While Keeping People Over 60: Creating Community Across Generations.* TCP Books, 2015.

Harvey, Jerry PhD. *The Abilene Paradox and Other Meditations on Management.* Lexington, Mass: Lexington Books, 1988.

Jones, Laurie Beth. *Jesus, Entrepreneur: Using Ancient Wisdom to Launch and Live Your Dreams.* New York: Three Rivers Press, 2001.

Kanoy, Liz. Senior Editor, Salem Web Network

Lucado, Max. *In the Grip of Grace.* Dallas, 1996. *Cure for the Common Life,* Nashville: Thomas Nelson, 2005

Lupton, Robert D. *Toxic Charity: How Churches and Charities Hurt Those They Help (and How to Reverse It).* New York: Harper One, 2011. *Charity Detox: What Charity Would Look Like if We Cared About Results.* New York: Harper One, 2015.

MacArthur, Dr. John. *Joy Rules.*

Malek, Sam. Creator of More Than Coffee, St. Louis, MO

McKie, Nathan W. Sr. *The Dignity of Profit: Creating Community with Entrepreneurship.* Maitland, FL: Kravitz and Sons LLC, 2025

Mises, Ludwig Von. *The Anti-capitalistic Mind.* 1956.

Murray, Andrew. Dutch Reformed Church missionary to South Africa

Palotta, Dan. http://www.ted.com/talks/. dan_palotta_the_way_we_think_about_charity_is_dead_wrong.

Pascal, Blaise. https://en.wikipedia.org/wiki/Pascal%27s_Wager

Peters, Tom. *A Passion for Excellence: The Leadership Difference.* Random House, 1985.

Porter, William Sydney (O.Henry). . *The Gift of the Magi,* 1905

Ramsey, Dave. EntreLeadership: 20 Years of Practical Business Wisdom from the Trenches, Howard Books 2011

Rodgers, Brenda. *Impact My Life: Biblical Mentoring Simplified.* Ebook 2014 Brenda Rodgers.

Schalk, Christoph. National Church Development

Schwarz, Christian. *The 3 Colors of Your Ministry.* St. Charles, IL: ChurchSmart Resources, 2001.

Sheldon, Charles. In His Steps (Abridged Christian Classics) Barbour Publishing, Inc. 2010

Smick, David M. *The Great Equalizer: How Main Street Capitalism Can Create an Economy for Everyone.* Philadelphia: Perseus Books, 2017

Stanley, Dr. Charles, 2008. https://www.intouch.org/

Swindoll, Charles (Chuck). Evangelical pastor, author, education, and radio preacher. Founder of Insight for Living ministries.

Tada, Joni Eareckson. *A Lifetime of Wisdom: Embracing the Way God Heals You.* Grand Rapids: Zondervan, 2009.

Thoreau, Henry David. American essayist, poet, philosopher, abolitionist, naturalist, tax resister, development critic, surveyor, and historian. 1817-1862.

Tobak, Steve. *What Makes a Successful Entrepreneur: Perseverance.*

Tozer, A. W. American Christian pastor, author, magazine editor, and spiritual mentor.

Tutu, Desmond. South African Anglican cleric and theologian.

Warren, Rick. The Purpose-Driven Life: What on Earth Am I Here For? Zondervan 2013

Wesley, John. 1703-1791. a leader of a revival movement within the Church of England known as Methodism.

Wilson, Larry. *Changing the Game: The New Way to Sell.* Touchstone, 1988

Zimbardo, Philip. *The Lucifer Effect: Understanding How Good People Turn Evil. New York:* Random House, 2007.